The
Cocker
Spaniel
Handbook

D. Caroline Coile, Ph.D.

With Full-color Photographs
Drawings by Michele Earle-Bridges

P9-DDF-899

BARRON'S

Acknowledgments
The author is indebted to the many Cocker Spaniel own-ers and breeders who contributed information and tips, and to her editors, Seymour Weiss and Annemarie McNamara for bringing it all together.

About the Author
Caroline Coile is an award-winning author who has writ-ten numerous articles about dogs for both scientific and lay publications. Her writing credits also include many well-respected books on the various aspects of dogs and dog sports. She holds a Ph.D. in neuroscience and behavior with special interests in canine sensory systems, genetics, and behavior. An active dog fancier since 1963, her own dogs have been nationally ranked in conformation, obedience, and performance activities.

Cover Credits
All cover photos are by Isabelle Francais.

Photo Credits
Norvia Behling: 9, 15, 34, 36, 37, 40, 54, 56, 71, and 92; Kent Dannen: 11, 17, 29, 42, 72, 78, 81, 97, 108, 118, 124, 125, 131, 140, and 147; Tara Darling: 5, 6, 39, 62, 94, 106, 127, 134, 136, 144, and 152; Shirley Fernandez: 44, 45, and 101; Isabelle Francais: vi, 2, 8, 13, 19, 20, 21, 25, 26, 38, 43, 53, 57, 69, 79, 82, 83, 84, 104, 110, 115, 122, 128, 139, 142, and 149; Daniel Johnson: 59, 65, 90, and 145; Pets by Paulette: 10, 16, 22, 27, 30, 48, 51, 60, 67, 68, 98, and 112.

Text © Copyright 2007 by D. Caroline Coile, Ph.D.
Illustrations © Copyright 2007 by Barron's Educational Series, Inc.

All inquiries should be addressed to:
Barron's Educational Series, Inc.
250 Wireless Boulevard
Hauppauge, New York 11788
http://www.barronseduc.com

ISBN-13: 978-0-7641-3459-3
ISBN-10: 0-7641-3459-0

Library of Congress Catalog Card No. 2006012576

Library of Congress Cataloging-in-Publication Data
Coile, D. Caroline.
The cocker spaniel handbook / D. Caroline Coile ; with full-color photographs.
  p. cm.
Includes index.
ISBN-13: 978-0-7641-3459-3
ISBN-10: 0-7641-3459-0
1. Cocker spaniels. I. Title.

SF429.C55C63 2006
636.752′4—dc22   2006012576

Printed in China
9 8 7 6 5 4 3 2 1

Important Note
This pet handbook gives advice to the reader on how to buy or adopt, and care for a Cocker Spaniel. The author and publisher consider it important to point out that the advice given in this book applies to normally developed puppies or adult dogs acquired from recog-nized dog breeders or adoption sources, dogs that have been examined and are in excellent physical health with good temperament.

Anyone who adopts a fully grown dog should be aware that the animal has already formed its basic impressions of human beings and their customary actions. The new owner should watch the animal care-fully, especially its attitude and behavior toward humans. If possible, the new owner should meet the previous owner before adopting the dog. If the dog comes from a shelter, the new owner should make an effort to obtain information about the dog's background, personality, and any individual peculiarities. Dogs coming from abu-sive homes or from homes in which they have been treated abnormally may react to handling in an unnatural manner, and they may have a tendency to snap or bite. Such dogs should only be adopted by people experi-enced with handling canine behavior problems.

Caution is further advised in the association of chil-dren with dogs, both puppies and adults, and in meeting other dogs, whether on or off leash.

Even well-behaved and carefully supervised dogs sometimes do damage to someone else's property or cause accidents. It is therefore in the owner's interest to be adequately insured against such eventualities, and we strongly urge all dog owners to purchase a liability policy that covers the dog.

Contents

Chapter One

Spaniels Span the Centuries

The Cocker Spaniel can't claim to be one of the oldest breeds, but it does come from a family with age-old roots. At least by ancient Roman times small dogs were used to drive and flush birds either into nets or into the air for falcons to pursue. These dogs may have been the ancestors of the spaniels that subsequently appeared in Europe.

The Spaniel Story

It is generally accepted that the word spaniel comes from *espagnol*, meaning "Spaniard," but a few historians disagree, pointing out that there is no evidence that Spain developed any spaniels. They suggest that instead the word may be derived from the Italian *spianare* or the French *espanir*, meaning "to flatten out" or "to get out of a net."

The earliest use of the word spaniel in reference to a dog occurs in King Howell the Good's Welsh Laws of A.D. 914. One of the earliest

Spaniels are an ancient family.

prints depicting spaniel-like dogs is from the 1300s; it shows them springing into the air to flush birds into flight, where a falcon awaits. This hunting technique is confirmed in later descriptions of spaniel sport.

The classic French text *Livre de chasse* (*Book of Hunting*), written in 1387, as well as its translation (with additions), *Master of the Game*, written between 1406 and 1413, mention spaniels. The text describes them as "spaniels, for their kind cometh from Spain, notwithstanding that there are many in other countries." It states that a good spaniel should not be "too rough," but "his tail should be rough." The spaniels commonly "go before their master, running and wagging their tail, and raise or start fowl and wild beasts. But their right craft is of the partridge, and of the quail." It continues, "when they be taught to be couchers, they be good to take partridges and quail with a net." The text concludes with some bad points, however, stating that spaniels "bark and goad" other dogs "if he sees geese or kine or horses, or hens, or oxen or other beasts." It finally cautions that unless the hunter has a falcon or goshawk

The Spaniel, the King, and the Pope

Legend has it that a spaniel played a role in England's split from the Roman Catholic Church beginning in 1534. Henry VIII wanted to divorce Catherine of Aragon, so he sent an ambassador to Rome to seek permission from Pope Clement VII. The ambassador, Lord Wiltshire, brought along his spaniel, which promptly bit the pope's toe while Wiltshire was kneeling. The pope sent Wiltshire home without the divorce consent, and Henry VIII formed the Church of England.

or a net, it would be best to do without them.

Geoffrey Chaucer also mentions spaniels in his prologue to "The Wife of Bath's Tale" in *Canterbury Tales*, written around the 1390s. The passage reads, "For as a Spaniel, she wol on him lepe."

Dame Juliana Berners, in her treatise on hunting in the *Boke of St. Albans*, published in 1486, mentioned spaniels in what was the first list of recognized breeds to be printed in English. "Thyse ben the names of houndes," she wrote, "fyrste there is a Grehoun, a Bastard, a Mengrell, a Mastiff, a Lemor, a Spanyel, Raches, Kenettys, Teroures, Butchers' Houndes, Myddyng dogges, Tryndeltaylles, and Prikherid currys, and smalle ladyes' poppees that bere aweye the flees."

The earliest attempt at a complete classification of dogs was published in 1570 as *De Canibus Britannicus*, by Dr. Johannes Caius. It included spaniels in the group called *Aucupatorii*, made up of dogs of the so-called "gentle kinde, serving the game." Caius stated that spaniels were mostly white, but that there were also a few red spaniels and black spaniels.

In 1621 Gervase Markham mentioned the setting spaniel in *The Art of Fowling*, stating that although many types of dogs can be taught to hunt birds, "yet is there none so excellent indeede as the true bred

Spaniels have adapted throughout history to different jobs and countries.

Land Spaniell, being of a nimbler and good size, rather small than grosse, and of a courageous and fierie mettall, evermore loving and desiring toyle." He mentions that while some believed certain colors superior to others, he considers the "Motley, the Liver-hude, or the White and Blacke spotted" equally good.

The next important attempt to classify dogs was by the Swedish naturalist Carolus Linnaeus in the mid-1700s. He gave spaniels their own category, along with the Latin names *Canis extratius*/*Canis hyspanicus*. This was followed by Buffon's taxonomy, which divided spaniels into Large Spaniels and Small Spaniels. The 1791 Dublin edition of the *Encyclopaedia Britannica* listed spaniels as one of dogdom's five main classes.

All Sorts of Spaniels

Spaniels came in a range of sizes and propensities, and hunters took advantage of this beginning at least by the late seventeenth century, breeding spaniels that specialized in either water or land hunting. Water spaniels flushed and retrieved waterfowl. Land spaniels flushed birds and rabbits on land, first finding them, then creeping forward to point and flush them out. With the advent of flintlocks

Spaniels are one of the oldest families of dogs developed to hunt in concert with humans.

First Spaniel in America?
When the *Mayflower* landed at Plymouth Rock in 1620, two dogs were on the passenger list: a mastiff and a spaniel.

for shooting, the role of the spaniel changed from flushing birds into nets or the air to pointing first. Woodcocks were often found in dense cover and required a smaller land spaniel to get in close. The English artist Thomas Bewick mentions the Cocker by name in 1790, and during the next ten years it appears to have earned a reputation distinct from that of other spaniels. In 1800 it is mentioned that the Duke of

Cocker Classes

Early Cocker fanciers needed to keep abreast of the changing class requirements. The following class divisions applied to Cockers at the Westminster Kennel Club:
• 1879: Cocker Spaniels and Field Spaniels were shown together.
• 1881: Cockers were separated from Field Spaniels by size, with Cockers designated as males under 28 pounds and females under 25 pounds.
• 1882: Black Cocker Spaniels under 28 pounds and Cocker Spaniels (other than black) under 28 pounds.
• 1883: Cocker Spaniels (black or black and white) under 28 pounds and Cocker Spaniels (other than black) under 28 pounds.
• 1884: Cocker Spaniels (liver or black) under 28 pounds and Cocker Spaniels (any color other than liver or black) under 28 pounds.
• 1889: Cocker Spaniels (black) and Cocker Spaniels (other than black).
• 1899: The designations ASCOB (Any Solid Color Other than Black). and Parti-color appear for the first time but are not separated.

Marlborough kept Cockers, which were described as "red and white with very round heads, blunt noses, a variety highly valued by sportsmen."

In his 1803 book *The Sportsman's Cabinet,* the British naturalist William Taplin said of them: "The smaller is called the cocker or cocking-spaniel, as being more adapted to covert and woodcock shooting, to which they are more particularly appropriated and by nature seem designed." The author compares Cockers to Springers by stating that "the cocker differs, having a shorter, more compact form, a rounder head, shorter nose, ears long (and the longer the more admired), the limbs short and strong, the coat more inclined to curl than the springer's." The Cocker's colors are described as liver and white, red, red and white, black and white, all liver, and not infrequently, black, with tanned muzzle and legs. The breed's attributes as a house dog are also first mentioned here; Cockers are described as having remarkable sagacity, fidelity, and gratitude, with "unwearied" attention and a zeal "above suspicion" to protect their masters' property.

Cocker Spaniels and dogs classified as Field Spaniels could come from the same litter; not only that, but the same dog could pass from one designation to another as it grew. This created a problem when grouping dogs for show purposes. Dogs under 25 pounds (or 28 pounds, depending on the year) were shown as Cockers, and those over that weight as Field Spaniels. A dog could be shown as a Cocker at one show and as a Field Spaniel at another a few months later if he just gained a little weight.

Several important events occurred in the late 1800s that shaped the future of the Cocker Spaniel:

The Cocker Spaniel was developed as a small land spaniel capable of locating and flushing woodcock from dense cover.

• 1878: "Capt" (or "Captain"), a liver and white, became the first Cocker Spaniel to be registered with the American Kennel Club.

• 1879: Obo, a dog often considered to be the first modern Cocker Spaniel, was born in England.

• 1881: The American Spaniel Club, the parent club of the Cocker Spaniel, was established. It was initially called the American Cocker Spaniel Club.

• 1882: A breeder in New England imported a female in whelp to Obo. One of the males from the resulting litter, Obo II, is credited as the father of Cockers in America.

• 1883: The Kennel Club in England began registering Cocker Spaniels as a distinct breed.

• 1885: The Spaniel Club (England) created the first breed standard for Cockers.

• 1892: The Kennel Club in England officially recognized Cocker Spaniels.

Cockers in America

The early 1900s saw an increase in the Cocker Spaniel's popularity in America. In 1921 a black parti-color female named Ch. Midkiff Seductive won Best in Show at the Westminster

who is sometimes credited as the father of the American Cocker Spaniel. From his litter came one of the most important Cockers of all time, Red Brucie. Red Brucie inherited his sire's longer legs, shorter back, and longer neck, and he passed these to his offspring. Although he never finished his championship, he was the most sought-after and successful Cocker stud of his day, siring 38 champions in his lifetime.

Kennel Club Dog Show, effectively crowning the Cocker as a major contender in such competitions.

Robinhurst Foreglow became an influential sire during this time. He was shorter-backed and longer-legged than most Cockers of the day, and his owner was so sure he could improve the breed that he offered the dog at stud free of charge. Many Cocker breeders declined, but two of the most prominent bred to him with history-making results. One of those breeders was Herman Mellenthin,

Of those champions, the single male pup from Brucie's last litter, Ch. My Own Brucie, was the unquestionable star. Mellenthin had been saving the Brucie name for a special dog, but when his friends saw the black puppy he had chosen to carry on his sire's name, they were stunned. To them he was gawky, chicken-necked, and big-headed. His show career started slowly, but eventually he proved them all wrong. He won Best in Show at the Morris & Essex Kennel Club Show, a competition second only to Westminster in prestige. Not content to win at the second-most prestigious show, the following year, 1940, Ch. My Own Brucie added Best in Show at Westminster to his laurels. Just to prove it was no fluke, he repeated his Westminster Best in Show win in 1941.

The War Effort

Although not as popular as German Shepherds and other larger dogs for war purposes, Cocker Spaniels were sometimes used as mine detectors during World War II.

He is one of only three dogs in history to win three Group firsts at Westminster (his other was in 1939). Brucie (as he was also called) became a celebrity and was featured in newsreels, movie shorts, and newspaper and magazine articles. He even had a full page in *Life* magazine. He became a household name, and everybody wanted a dog just like him. When Brucie died, in 1943 at age eight, *The New York Times* carried his obituary; the *New York Sun*'s front-page obituary was headlined "Noted Cocker Spaniel Dies."

The English-American Split

Cockers in America gradually diverged from their English ancestors, becoming smaller but with proportionally longer legs, and more elegant. This American type predominated in show rings both in numbers and awards, so that the old-fashioned English type had difficulty competing against them. Some fanciers of the English type gave up on showing and turned the dogs to field work instead. In 1935 separate classes for the two types were introduced, but a dog could be entered in either. At least one American Cocker finished its championship entirely from within the English Cocker class.

The English Cocker Spaniel Club of America was formed in 1935, adopting the standard in use in England at that time. By 1938 the

The English Cocker (above right) is longer-legged and has a more rectangular head and shorter coat compared to the American version (below right).

The ASCOB variety, which was designated as a separate variety in 1944, stands for "Any Solid Color Other than Black," and includes the popular buffs.

club resolved that members would not interbreed English with American Cockers. They defined English Cockers as those whose pedigrees could be traced in all lines to dogs registered with the English Kennel Club by January 1, 1930.

Mrs. Geraldine R. Dodge, an eminent dog fancier and president of the club, researched pedigrees in order to separate English from American Cockers, and presented those findings in 1941. In 1946 the American Kennel Club (AKC) agreed to recognize two distinct breeds: the Cocker Spaniel and the English Cocker Spaniel. Note that only in America are these designations used; in Britain and the rest of the world the two breeds are known as the American Cocker Spaniel and the Cocker Spaniel.

Cockers in the Field

The first official spaniel field trial in any country was held in England in 1899. The winner was a dog named Stylish Pride. The first field trial for Cockers in America was held in 1924, although accounts of the time noted that none of the entrants had even been trained! Interest and knowledge grew, however, so that by the next year the Hunting Cocker Spaniel Club drew an entry of 22 Cockers.

Cocker Celebrities

• Spot, of the *Fun with Dick and Jane* primers, introduced millions of schoolchildren to Cocker Spaniels. Although the original 1930s Spot was a terrier, by 1940 he was a black parti Cocker.

• Cover Boy Butch was known as the model for many magazine covers drawn by Albert Staehl. The black parti made his first of 25 appearances on the cover of the *Saturday Evening Post* in 1944. He was usually depicted engaging in some sort of mischief, in this case chewing up a book of wartime rationing stamps. Readers deluged the *Post* with letters defending the puppy. The magazine knew it had a hit, and Butch and Butch, Jr., appeared on its covers for 20 years.

• Lady, of the 1955 Disney animated movie, *Lady and the Tramp*, helped many families fall in love with Cockers. The movie was the romantic tale of a pampered buff Cocker Spaniel and a streetwise mutt.

• Champion Dog Prince Tom was the hero of a children's book of the same name published in 1958. It was the story of a Cocker who became a National Field Trial Champion.

• The Coppertone Cocker, shown pulling the bathing suit off a young girl and exposing her tan line in an advertisement for a brand of suntan lotion, was modeled after the artist's neighbor's black Cocker.

In 1953 the American Spaniel Club offered a National Cocker Championship, open to both English and American Cockers. English Cockers won the first few years, but in 1956 a buff American Cocker, Prince Tom III U.D., became the first of his breed (as well as the first obedience-titled and first amateur-handled Cocker) to win a National. In 1957 another American Cocker, the black Field Ch. Berol Lodge Glen Garry, topped the competition. American Cockers were also the victors in 1960 and 1961, but entries ultimately declined so much in the 1960s that the events were discontinued by 1964.

In 1977 the ASC initiated its Working Dog and Working Dog Excellent Programs, and in 1988 the American Kennel Club began offering Spaniel Hunting Tests, encouraging owners

Cockers had no qualms about moving from the field to the couch and becoming America's number one dog.

Cockers of all varieties have been famous, but perhaps it was the black "Spot" who, as Dick and Jane's companion, introduced most youngsters to the breed.

to field-train their Cockers The first Cocker field trial in thirty years was held in 1993, and since then interest has continued to grow. In 1998 the National Field Trial Championship for Cocker Spaniels and English Cockers was once again a reality. At first taking place only every other year, in 2003 it became an annual event.

The Spaniel Spell

The year 1940 was significant in Cocker history not only because of Brucie's win at Westminster, but also because by then the Cocker Spaniel had risen to become the most popular breed in America, holding that top spot from 1940 to 1952. Even splitting the breed in 1946 didn't pull down the registration numbers significantly, since the English Cockers were but a small proportion of the total. In 1952 Cockers were overtaken in popularity as a breed but still hovered near number one, reclaiming their title as America's favorite in 1984. They held on to their crown until 1990. Since then the Cocker's popularity has declined, although it is still one of the most beloved of all breeds. The Cocker Spaniel was fifteenth in AKC registrations for 2005, with more than 16,000 registered in that year.

Many, if not most, responsible Cocker breeders see the decline in popularity as a welcome event. Although it's nice to have a breed that everybody likes, that popularity attracts people who don't have its best interests in mind. Because the Cocker Spaniel is relatively easy to breed, anyone with a pen out back could get some dogs and start selling puppies. The people who bought those puppies in turn often decided to breed the next generation, and soon the Cocker population was overwhelmed by dogs raised by owners with no idea of proper type or temperament, and no conception of how to avoid health problems. As a result, the breed's quality plummeted. Cockers that snapped at children gave the breed a bad reputation, and a bevy of Cocker health problems proliferated. As with other popular dogs, Cockers fell victim to impulse purchasing; when buyers ignorant of the breed's needs and problems figured out that a Cocker Spaniel wasn't always an angel, more and more ended up in shelters and rescue. That the Cocker clung to its spot at or near the top for

Cockers remain one of America's favorite dogs.

so many years is a testament to its appeal and resilience.

Now that the Cocker Spaniel's popularity has waned, many so-called breeders looking only to make a buck have largely moved on to other dogs, although plenty of puppy millers and naïve backyard breeders remain. Many Cockers are still abandoned or given to rescue. Serious breeders hope that the Cocker's favor will fall to the point that prospective owners will make the effort to educate themselves about the breed before acquiring a dog, and that they will know how to find a Cocker with the best chance of having the proper health and temperament.

Chapter Two
Fine Feathered Friends

Cockers didn't sit in the top spot of popularity for more than a quarter of a century without good reason. What is it about Cockers that have made them America's sweethearts for so long? What is it about Cockers that may make one the perfect match for you? And how do you find that perfect match among all the Cocker litters out there?

What's Special About Spaniels?

Spaniels are the jacks-of-all-trades of the sporting-dog world. They find, flush, and retrieve birds. Watching a Cocker quarter a field, zigzagging back and forth about thirty feet in front of his handler, eyes, ears, and especially nose ready for the slightest hint of bird, is awe-inspiring. Although comparatively few people today choose a Cocker for his hunting prowess, that birdiness is what shaped this smallest Sporting breed.

Originally Cockers were favored as hunting companions. That changed as the breed rocketed to the top of the popularity charts, when the Cocker gained renown as a competitive show dog and extraordinary companion. The breed became more extreme in conformation, sporting a coat of extreme beauty but too long to be functional for field work (or easy home care); the dog's reputation as a hunter was replaced by its status as a family dog. The Cocker's popularity attracted unscrupulous and careless breeders who allowed bad traits to multiply. Although puppy millers of this type have not been eliminated, dedicated breeders have largely corrected many of the dog's physical and behavioral problems.

Personality plus: The breed is known as the "merry" Cocker for good reason. The Cocker Spaniel is an eternal optimist. His tail is a perpetual blur of wagging activity. He's eager to go on a run in the field, a jaunt around the block, and a ride to town. He's just as eager to play a game in the yard, snooze beside you on the couch, or learn a new trick.

The Cocker is a lover, not a fighter. He loves people, other pets, other dogs, and children. But he does need socialization in order to be all that he can be. Cockers are

actually quite sensitive, and they can become wary of people if they don't grow up knowing that strangers, including children, are generally kind. Unfortunately, too many are never exposed to strangers except for visits to the veterinarian, where they get an injection, and to the groomer, where their coat is pulled during detangling. They grow to dread meeting new people because so far, those encounters have been painful. Add to that Cockers with inborn temperament problems, and you may have a dog that snaps when approached by strangers. Careful selection of puppies from responsible breeders, along with careful socialization, usually negates this possible downside.

The Cocker's sensitive nature can also lead to behavioral problems. He is quick to pick up on the moods of his people. Unhappy and argumentative families can cause him to become stressed. He must be handled gently and calmly; this is not a breed that needs to be shown who's boss. Rough or callous treatment tends to make the Cocker withdraw. When trained with a soft hand and lots of rewards, the Cocker can excel as an obedient companion.

A Cocker expects to be a real member of the family, involved in everything the rest of the family does. He cannot be relegated to the backyard, garage, or laundry room, where he would languish from loneliness. He's eager to help—or at least be underfoot—as you cook dinner, do the laundry, and run errands.

Some Cockers are barkers. Training can help teach them when barking is acceptable, but if you are bark-intolerant, then be careful that you choose a Cocker from quiet parents. Cockers can be alert watchdogs, but don't count on one to fend off attackers. They were never bred to be protection dogs, and most do not understand the concept.

Size: As the smallest Sporting breed, the Cocker has a distinct advantage when it comes to the fine art of lap sitting and sofa sharing. Small dogs are not only easier to cuddle; they are easier to live with. They cost less to feed, house, and

Cocker IQ Tests

One of most famous studies of dog genetics and behavior was performed by John Scott and John Fuller in the 1950s and '60s. Among the five breeds they compared on various behavior tasks was the Cocker Spaniel. Their findings showed that you can't claim that one breed is smarter than another based on just one test. Each breed was best at different types of learning tasks, usually those types that involved something the breed was originally bred to do. For example, on a task that required puppies to remain still for a minute while being weighed, the Cockers were the champs, with 70 percent being able to stay still, as compared to only 10 percent of the worst breed tested. In general, for tests involving restraint, Cocker Spaniels did best. This may reflect the Cocker's hunting ability to show restraint and freeze upon finding a bird before flushing it. This may also explain why Cockers overwhelmingly surpassed the others at a test of delayed response, in which they had to remember a cue and then wait for some time before having the chance to respond to it—just as they might have to do when marking a bird's fall before retrieving it.

Cocker Spaniels also outshone most of the other breeds when it came to traversing a raised plank to get to food. But they were the very worst of the breeds at a task that required them to use their paws to uncover a dish of food. In fact, they were the worst at any task that required them to manipulate objects, including moving a dish or pulling a string. Cockers cannot be accused of being manipulative!

board, and travel well. You can even find lots of high-fashion outfits and luxury beds unavailable for larger breeds. Yet Cockers are large enough to accompany you jogging and partake in any big-dog activity.

In summary:

• If you have your heart set on a good dog with which to share a casual day of upland game hunting, a Cocker will do fine. If your sights are set on a top field-trial dog, though, you might do better with another spaniel.

• If you dream of having the most beautiful dog on the block, then choose a Cocker. If you want to compete in the beauty pageant of dog shows, you may find the Cocker a difficult breed to start with because of the precise grooming required and top-notch competition in the ring.

• If you enjoy training a quick study, you'll enjoy the Cocker. If you plan to compete seriously in obedience trials, expect to work a little harder than owners of more traditional obedience breeds.

Cockers are lovers, not fighters.

• If running and jumping with your dog over a doggy agility course sounds like fun, you can reach the heights with your Cocker. If you want to be among the fastest runners, the Cocker probably won't get you across the finish line first.

• If sharing a fulfilling life with a loyal, intelligent, beautiful jack-of-all-trades dog is really what you have in mind, you won't do better than a Cocker Spaniel.

Cocker Commitments

Cockers have it all when it comes to take-me-home appeal: a fun-loving personality, an athletic form, a luxurious coat, big floppy ears, and melting puppy-dog eyes. And every one of them means extra work for you.

Extra Exercise

You may think of energetic play as a video game marathon, and of a marathon as a walk around the block, but your Cocker Spaniel has other ideas. He's a sporting dog through and through. He was made to keep going and going, ranging across fields, pushing through brush, sniffing out hidden birds, and retrieving downed birds. A Cocker Spaniel that called it quits after a quick romp would find himself out of the gene pool in short order. That means your Cocker-to-be comes from a pedigree of high-energy, high-stamina ancestors, and chances are, he's ready to follow in their tracks.

Most new dog owners tend to overestimate the time they have to spend with a dog. They start with a bang, but as the excitement wears off, walks are shortened and outings are postponed. The dog gets frus-

Their easygoing attitude and fun-loving spirit make Cockers good companions for responsible young people.

trated from lack of mental and physical stimulation, and tries to compensate by chewing, digging, barking, and generally running amuck. His owner thinks the dog is hyperactive, but he's not. He is a normally active Cocker Spaniel stuck with a hypoactive human.

Optimally you should plan on spending an hour with your dog three times a day. Realistically, that's not going to happen because you need to make a living. If you work, plan on getting up an hour earlier than usual (don't worry; your Cocker will wake you up while it's still dark) so you can squeeze in a morning exercise session. Then plan on spending at least an hour—preferably more—in the afternoon. Exercise includes running, retrieving, swimming, and mental workouts such as mind games, agility

tests, and training. Hunting is always the favored exercise.

You don't need an estate for your Cocker. Many Cockers do well as apartment dwellers, or with small yards. The secret is that their owners make the effort to spend lots of quality time with their dogs. They play mental games and fetch games indoors, take long walks on leash, and interact when they are home together.

Extra Training

Cockers are eager to learn, and if you don't oblige them, they will teach themselves—and you may not like what's in the Cocker curriculum. These are active, people-oriented dogs, and unless you focus their energy and intelligence, they are sure to get into mischief. Give your Cocker the extra training he needs, and you will be rewarded many times over.

Extra Coat Care

Not only is the Cocker coat long, it's also extremely thick and full. Many Cockers have hair that tangles and mats easily, and regardless of coat type, dirty coats or coats with debris in them will mat quickly. Maintaining a Cocker coat requires diligence. Plan on spending a half hour three times a week combing and brushing, making sure that you reach all the way to the skin, where mats can hide. You will also need to pick or comb burrs and twigs out of the coat as soon as they get tangled in it. The feet, which are profusely coated, track in sand, mud, leaves, and whatever else they sweep up on the way to your door.

Mats are more than unsightly; they continue to recruit more hair, eventually pulling the dog's skin and becoming uncomfortable. They can form a protective roof over parasite infestations and moist skin conditions, allowing itchy infections to form. Dematting is a time-consuming process that can be painful for your dog. If you cannot devote the time to keeping your Cocker's coat mat-free, arrange to have the coat clipped close.

That's not all. Your Cocker will need trimming; otherwise, he will look like a ragamuffin. Trimming requires skill. You can develop this skill, but it will take time, effort, and a lot of mistakes. Most people choose instead to have their Cocker professionally groomed once every four to six weeks. Depending on where you live, this costs about $50 per visit. Cockers groomed for the show ring require hours of thinning and shaping in order to achieve a natural, blended look to the coat. Grooming shops will instead clip the hair over most of the body. It won't look as natural, and the hair will feel softer after being clipped, but the savings in time will be well worth any small differences in appearance. You can also opt for a short allover haircut, keeping coat care to a minimum.

Cockers have fleshy lips that tend to have folds that can remain moist. These moist areas are perfect havens in which bacteria can multiply, causing skin infections. You will need to keep any lip folds clean and dry.

True to their hunting dog heritage, Cockers love the outdoors and need ample chance to exercise.

Extra Ear Care

The Cocker's gorgeous big hanging ears, so abundantly covered in hair, have a downside: They allow ear infections to thrive in the warm, moist environment of the ear canal. Once an infection is established, it can be difficult to get it cleared up. Cocker ears can become terribly inflamed, prompting the dog to scratch at them and shake his head over and over until he creates further damage, often breaking blood vessels inside the ear flap and causing a hematoma. Cockers with painful ears have been known to bite when provoked. Who can blame them? You will need to check and perhaps clean your Cocker's ears several times a week. You may also need to fasten

17

your Cocker's ears back or up to allow air to circulate in the canal.

You must take special care of the outside of your Cocker's ears as well. Especially if allowed to grow long, the hair on the ears extends beyond a Cocker's short muzzle when he lowers his head to eat or drink. That means his ears end up sopping up water, and worse, getting gummed up with food. They can also get into your Cocker's mouth, where he is likely to just chew off the offending hair. You can easily solve this problem by having your Cocker wear a snood, or band of material around his ears, while he eats. Alternatively, you can simply feed and water him from a deep, narrow bowl that allows his ears to fall on either side of the bowl.

Extra Eye Care

Cockers have a reputation for eye problems. You will need to keep an eye on your dog's eyes to make sure errant hairs, lashes, or whiskers are not touching the cornea and causing irritation. Cockers with lid problems may need special care to keep hair away from the eye or to keep the eyes free of foreign objects

Many eye problems cause a watery or mucous discharge. Some Cockers have tear ducts that fail to open (a condition called *imperforate lacrimal punctum*), so their tears drain out onto the face. Tears stain the coat red. You will need to keep the eyes clean to make your Cocker comfortable and attractive. You may also need to keep the face wiped clean to try to prevent tearstains.

Extra Time

Cockers have a typical lifespan of from 12 to 15 years. That's a long-term commitment to make—but not nearly long enough once you fall in love with this fine feathered friend.

Health Concerns

An unfortunate legacy of the Cocker's longtime popularity is the breed's reputation as repository of health problems. It's an undeserved reputation—but one with some basis in fact.

Founding Fathers— and Mothers

To understand breed-related health problems in dogs, you have to go back to breed origins. Every breed is founded on a small sample from the canine gene pool. It's postu-

The Cocker coat needs a lot of maintenance to look its best.

lated that every individual—whether human or canine—carries from four to seven recessive genes for serious health diseases. When you take a small sample of individuals, and then breed them only among themselves, you trap those bad genes (along with all the good ones) and they become part of the breed's gene pool. With such a limited gene pool, the chances of two carriers mating with each other are high, and that means there is a greater chance of producing affected offspring. Cockers are no exception here; like almost every breed of dog, they arrived on the scene with genetic baggage.

Problems and Popularity

When any breed of dog becomes popular, there are many more chances for affected offspring to be born simply because there are many more dogs. Even though the percentage of affected dogs may be low, their absolute numbers make the problem appear rampant. In fact, the problem is made worse by people who have no knowledge of genetics or health start breeding dogs, either just on a whim or to make money. Dogs that have hereditary defects and thus should not be bred instead produce litter after litter of carriers or affected offspring.

Cocker Spaniels were in the hands of such ill-informed and ill-intentioned breeders for many generations. Fortunately, by sheer chance, many Cockers emerged perfectly healthy. Other lines of Cockers remained in the hands of dedicated

Although Cockers are known for eye problems, careful screening of breeding stock has significantly reduced the prevalence of such problems in well-bred dogs.

breeders who never succumbed to the temptation of breeding for money. These dogs helped today's breeders restore the Cocker as the healthy breed it once was. Nonetheless, Cockers are still predisposed to a handful of health problems (see Chapter 9 for a complete description of these).

Eye problems. At the top of the problem list are eye problems. Cockers are one of many breeds that can have progressive retinal atrophy (PRA), a retinal disease that leads to blindness. An eye exam can detect it when the dog is about three to six years of age, or an electroretinogram

can detect it as young as one year of age. A DNA test is in development; the condition is recessively inherited.

Lid problems are also relatively common; the lids may turn in toward the eye (entropion), which can irritate the cornea, or out from it (ectropion), which predisposes the eye to infections. Extra lashes often grow toward the cornea, irritating it. Dry eye, in which tear production is inadequate, can cause discomfort, corneal scarring, and blindness. Cockers are also prone to glaucoma, juvenile cataracts, episcleritis, and cherry eye. You can hedge your bet by selecting puppies from stock in which as many relatives as possible have a Canine Eye Registration Foundation (CERF) clearance. These clearances are good for only one year, so your potential puppy's parents should have been cleared within the past year.

Ear problems. Ear problems seem to go with the breed. It's not just the big, heavy ears that don't allow air circulation. It's the hair that grows within the ear, and the fairly high sebum level within the canal. Your best bet is to choose parents with healthy ears and healthy skin. Why healthy skin? You will want that anyway, but the surface of the ear canal is an extension of the skin, and often skin and ear problems go hand in hand.

Skin problems. If relatives of your potential puppy scratch themselves frequently or have hair loss, you need to ask why. Allergies, seborrhea, and demodectic mange tend to have a hereditary influence, and can be difficult to treat. Allergies are the major cause of ear infections.

Skeletal problems. Cockers have two types of joint problems that are of concern. The first is patellar luxation, in which the knee cap slips out of place. Hip dysplasia, so common in many breeds, is not that common in Cockers. Screening tests and clearances exist for both conditions through the Orthopedic Foundation for Animals (OFA). About 6 percent of Cockers for which OFA data are available are dysplastic, which is far less than in most breeds. Because of that, not all breeders consider OFA hip clearances essential. However, it is certainly a good sign if they can provide them. In contrast, about 27 percent of Cockers listed in the OFA database have patellar luxation—the third-highest percentage of any breed. By choosing a pup with parents and a pedigree full of dogs with certified good knees and hips, you are bettering your dog's chances of having healthy joints.

Cockers are also susceptible to intervertebral disc disease, in which the cushioning discs between the bones of the spine collapse and allow the spinal cord to become pinched.

Autoimmune problems. Autoimmune problems, in which the body's immune system turns against some part of the self, are becoming more well known in many breeds. The extent to which they are hereditary is unknown, but it does seem that some autoimmune diseases are more prevalent in Cockers than in

A healthy Cocker can enjoy life to its fullest.

other breeds. These include immune-mediated hemolytic anemia (IMHA), in which the body attacks its own red blood cells, and some types of thyroid disease, leading to hypothyroid condition. Ask about the history of severe disease, such as IMHA. Ask about thyroid test results, which some breeders will have in the form of OFA clearances. Of the Cockers in the OFA database, about 7 percent have immune-mediated thyroiditis, a far lower number than in many other breeds.

Heart problems. Many breeds have hereditary heart problems. In Cockers, a form of dilated cardiomyopathy, a potentially fatal weakness of the heart muscle, appears to be breed related. This form is sometimes responsive to supplementation of taurine in the diet. Another cardiac

Cockers from parents that have been screened for genetic diseases have the best chance of growing up healthy.

condition, sick sinus syndrome, is a type of abnormal heart beating that results in low blood pressure, weakness, and fainting. Many breeders will have a heart clearance available for their breeding stock. The older the dog is when he is checked to be heart healthy, the better.

Phosphofructokinase deficiency (PFK). Canine phosphofructokinase deficiency is a condition that prevents metabolism of glucose into energy, and also destroys red blood cells. Affected dogs cannot tolerate exercise. The disease is caused by a recessive gene, and that gene probably occurs in about 10 percent of the population. Fortunately, a DNA test is available that can detect clear, carrier, and affected dogs. Avoid litters in which both parents are carriers or affected. If DNA results are not available for both parents, insist on having a sale pending a clear or carrier DNA status for your puppy. Carriers show no sign of the disease. The OFA maintains a registry of PFK DNA results for Cockers.

Neurological problems. As in so many breeds, Cockers seem prone to epilepsy. At this time the genetic nature of the problem is not known.

Cockers have also been labeled as one of the breeds susceptible to so-called rage syndrome. Rage syndrome is a controversial tag for dogs that seem to become suddenly aggressive without warning. Some breeders contend that these dogs show subtle warning signs, which owners neglect to see, and then the dog finally erupts. Others believe the condition is a type of epilepsy. Whatever the reason, some normally mellow and sweet Cockers have been known to attack suddenly and ferociously. The condition is extremely rare and your best bet is to question the breeder about the dog's temperament.

Blood-clotting disorders. Cockers, like many breeds, can develop blood-clotting disorders such as von Willebrand's disease; however, the condition is not common. Blood tests can determine if a dog is affected and to what degree. Another type of clotting disorder found in Cockers is factor-X deficiency, which causes severe bleeding in puppies but mild bleeding in adults. A blood test is available. It is thought to be inherited as a recessive.

Liver problems. Cockers have a greater than average incidence of chronic hepatitis and copper toxicosis. At this point little is known about the hereditary nature of these problems in Cockers.

Finding a healthy Cocker. No responsible breeder wants to produce unhealthy dogs. For this reason good breeders screen their breeding stock for as many hereditary Cocker problems as possible. They don't stop there, they also ask for health reports from owners of all the puppies they have produced in the past. By collecting as much information about not just the direct ancestors, but also about their siblings, breeders can become aware of health problems in the line.

There is no such thing as a line that has never produced a health problem. If one were to remove from the breeding pool every dog with a connection to a health problem, there would be no dogs left to breed. The best a breeder can do is try to avoid breeding likely carriers together. The best you can do is to find an honest breeder with a good grasp of genetics and a lot of health information.

Chapter Three

Cocker Choices

It's easy to find a Cocker Spaniel— but it's not the easy-to-find ones you want. You want a Cocker bred by somebody who is careful about the dogs he or she breeds, about the way they are raised, and about the homes they go to. Such breeders don't always make themselves easy to find because they often already have a waiting list of good homes. You can get on that list, but you have to demonstrate that you are as dedicated an owner as he or she is a breeder.

Looking for Love

An excellent place to start is the American Spaniel Club (ASC) breeder referral list, available online at *www.asc-cockerspaniel.org* listed under the menu button for "Cocker Info." These breeders are all members of the American Spaniel Club, and have agreed to abide by the club's code of ethics. You can also get the names of local Cocker clubs from the ASC, and through them meet local Cocker breeders and learn of local events. You can also find good breeders at dog shows, field tri-

als, in Cocker Spaniel magazines, and in all-breed dog magazines such as *Dog World*. You can join one of the many Cocker Spaniel discussion lists and get to know breeders there. You can also find breeders on the Internet, but you must evaluate them carefully. The newspaper is seldom a reliable source of good dogs or breeders.

Choose a Choosy Breeder

One way to evaluate breeders is to compare how they evaluate you. Good breeders are choosy about where their puppies go. They make sure their puppies will go to homes where they will be loved for a lifetime. They know that caring for a Cocker Spaniel requires a lot of commitment and work. They are too familiar with people who make big promises but are not really prepared for Cocker ownership. Good breeders will ask about your experience with dogs and with Cockers in particular. They will ask about your facilities and family. They will discuss expenses, exercise, training, grooming, health care, and safety issues with you. They may require that you neuter or spay your dog. They may ask you to wait for several months for a litter; during this "cooling off" period they can make sure you are not just impulse buying. If a breeder doesn't care where his or her puppies are going, they probably don't care where they came from either, and there's a good chance very little thought went into breeding and raising the litter.

Ask how many litters the breeder has each year. Breeders who always have puppies, or who have several different breeds, probably can't give each litter the attention it deserves. Ideally, you want your litter to grow up in the breeder's home, not in a kennel or garage.

Why do you want a good breeder? Besides being your best source of a puppy with good health, good temperament, and good looks, a good breeder will be a mentor and friend. You will always be able to ask questions, share anecdotes, and find help. You will find yourself part of an extended family of puppy owners, and you can keep up with littermates throughout their lives. Should circumstances arise that force you to surrender your dog, good breeders are there to make sure he is taken care of.

Pedigrees

What kind of family is your puppy from? Start by looking at pedigrees. Are the dogs AKC or UKC registered? No other registry in the United States is considered a serious registry of Cocker Spaniels. Are there titled dogs within the first three generations? (For a full list of titles, go to *www.akc.org*.) Titles can give you an

They may look alike at first glance, but all Cockers are not created equal.

idea not only of the quality of the pedigree, but of how serious the breeder is in producing superior puppies. Avoid inbred pedigrees; although many breeders practice inbreeding (in which the same dogs appear behind the sire and dam), the average pet owner has little to gain from an inbred dog. Inbreeding increases the chance of two recessive genes appearing in a puppy, at the risk of certain health problems.

Ask the breeder about health clearances of dogs in the pedigree. If the sire and dam have no clearances, look elsewhere. Avoid especially young parents; because most health problems appear in later

him. In fact, the breeder should have not only a pedigree of the litter available, but pictures of most of the dogs in it. If the breeder cannot tell you about the dogs in the pedigree, it suggests a lack of research, preparation, and knowledge.

Puppies!

Of course, you're there to see the puppies—and once you set eyes on those frolicking pups all your good sense will fly out the window. That's why you really should go home puppyless and make your final decision without those soulful eyes pleading with you. While you are with the pups, steel yourself to make an honest evaluation of them.

Cocker Spaniels are among dogdom's most adorable puppies. They sleep hard and play hard, so if they are sleeping, you may have to wait in order to see them at their best. They should be friendly toward you; avoid any that are shy or that are overly independent. Although their coats will be short, they should look like miniature Cockers even at a young age. Their eyes, ears, and nose should be free of discharge, and they should show no signs of diarrhea.

Make any sale contingent upon a veterinary examination within 48 hours. Your veterinarian is in the best position to evaluate the puppy's health. The breeder should have supplied the puppy's vaccinations and worming records.

years, young dogs may simply not be old enough to show the problems they may eventually develop.

Meet the Family

Once you have narrowed down your choices, try to visit in person. If the breeder does not allow visits, then look elsewhere. If he or she does, make sure the puppies are raised in a clean, healthy environment that allows them to interact with people. Get to meet the dam and other doggy family members, and make sure their temperaments are good. The sire may not be on the premises, but the breeder should have pictures and possibly videos of

The breeder can provide the best source of information about each puppy's personality.

What Age?

The best time to bring a new puppy home is between 8 and 12 weeks of age. Before 7 weeks, removing a puppy from its dam and littermates deprives it of learning essential canine social skills. After 12 weeks, puppies naturally become more fearful of new situations. However, especially if the breeder has taken measures to expose the puppy to new experiences and people, an older puppy can also make the transition just fine. Don't hesitate to welcome a well-adjusted Cocker of any age into your home. In fact, adult Cockers are a great choice if you value your furniture, rugs, and sanity.

Rescue

Cocker Spaniels find themselves homeless for many reasons. Most often it's just a case of the wrong home for the right dog. People who promised they would care for their Cocker for a lifetime got tired of the brushing and walking. They got fed up with behavior problems that they caused themselves by not properly exercising or training their dog. They may have welcomed a human baby into the family, and no longer had time for the Cocker they once called their baby. Sometimes people abandon a dog just because the animal gets old or develops health prob-

Short Tail, Long Tail?

Most Cockers in America have their tails docked within a few days of birth. Those born in other countries may have intact tails, depending upon that country's laws concerning docking. Some hunting breeds are customarily docked because they injure their tails with vigorous wagging while in the field, but this is not the case with most Cockers. If a dog goes beyond a few days of age without having the tail docked, the procedure requires general anesthesia. Most show dogs have docked tails; however, non–show-oriented veterinarians have a tendency to dock the tail too short for show. An experienced breeder should consult with the veterinarian before docking.

lems. Some Cockers are found roaming the streets. Sometimes Cocker owners sadly relinquish them because they lose their home, can't afford veterinary treatment, or have become too infirm themselves to care for them properly. Sometimes owners die without having made provisions for their Cocker.

Rescue Cockers come in all ages, from all circumstances, and in all conditions. Sometimes entire litters come to rescue, sometimes ancient dogs who seek only a secure home in which to spend their last days. Many rescues have been cherished companions and are suddenly alone in the world. Other rescues have never lived in a house before or known a gentle touch or kind word. Regardless, they are often apprehensive, confused, and even frightened. They may cling to their foster owners or new families, as though afraid they will lose their beacon of hope. With time, training, and security they gradually adapt to their new circumstances and become exceptional family companions.

Some prospective owners fear that adopting a rescue is just taking on somebody else's problem, or that rescue dogs come with emotional baggage. Such dogs are the exception. Rescue dogs have already had their hearts broken and need secure, permanent homes where it won't happen again. That's one reason rescue groups are picky about where these dogs go. Most begin the adoption process by having prospective homes complete an application. Applicants may be asked to provide veterinary references, and the rescue group may schedule a phone interview or home visit. Although this may seem invasive, it's partly to provide the best match of dog and situation.

Many rescue groups provide temperament testing, basic training, and behavior consultation. Adopting from a rescue group provides new owners with a safety net should problems arise. Many groups require adoptive owners to enroll in obedience classes in order to encourage bonding, basic dog training skills, and basic manners. They also often provide opportunities to become club members, participate in Cocker activ-

Parti-colors come in the same range of colors as the solids, but with white splashed over the base pattern. These are buff parti-colors.

ities and rescue reunions, and even become part of the rescue team.

Some people think that rescue dogs are free. They aren't. Not only do people tend to value objects or pets they have an investment in more than those they don't, but rescue groups need to charge a reasonable fee to recoup their expenses and continue to provide services. A rescue Cocker is the deal of a lifetime.

What Color Cocker?

The Cocker Spaniel is one of only two AKC breeds divided into varieties according to color. Dogs of one Cocker variety may be bred to those of another Cocker variety, and the offspring are registered according to their color variety rather than that of any parent. Different varieties do not compete against one another at all-breed dog shows, although the best of each variety at independent Cocker

Spaniel specialty shows may compete for Best of Breed. In Cockers the three varieties are black, parti-color, and ASCOB. The colors included within each variety go beyond those the variety names would suggest.

The Black Variety

Not surprisingly, the black variety includes all-black dogs. A small amount of white may be allowed on the throat or chest. The black variety also includes black and tan dogs, which are marked with typical tan points on the eyebrows, sides of the muzzle, under the ears, under the tail, on each foot, and partway up each leg, and sometimes on the chest.

The ASCOB Variety

ASCOB stands for Any Solid Color Other than Black. It includes cream, buff, red, brown, and all shades in between, with or without tan points, and with only a small amount of white allowable on the throat and chest.

Sable, in which each hair (most often red) is tipped with black, was once included in this variety but has since been disallowed in AKC Cockers. It is still an acceptable color in Canadian Cockers.

The Parti-color Variety

Add lots of white to either of the above varieties, and you have a parti-color. The white should make up at least 10 percent of the dog's coat. Tan points will be in the same places as in any tan-pointed dog. Roans, in which tiny flecks of color are interspersed with white, are included in this variety.

As a practical matter parti-colors are seldom crossed with either of the solid colored varieties because they often produce dogs with too much white to be considered solid and too little white to be considered partis. Dogs with less than 10 percent white, and with more than the small touches of white on the throat and chest, are disqualified according to the breed standard.

Color and Temperament

Many breeders believe the three varieties tend to have slightly different temperaments. The ASCOB, especially the buff, is labeled the wild child, less likely to excel at tasks involving rote obedience but always ready for fun. The black is said to be the sweetheart, most likely to snuggle and try to please. The parti-color is the alleged brains of the operation, but uses its smarts for mischief-making and clowning as often as for following orders.

Is there anything to these generalities? It's possible that relatively closed breeding populations could lead to slightly different temperaments, although there are plenty of dogs in each variety to disprove the theory. Maybe you'll have to get one of each and see for yourself.

Chapter Four

Starting Off with Your Spaniel

What takes years in human childhood takes only months in dog puppyhood. That means every day is that much more critical to your puppy's development. The next few months will make a huge impact on the quality of the many years you will share with your Cocker.

Countering Cocker Chaos

Getting ready for a new puppy is harder than getting ready for a new baby. Unlike a new baby, your Cocker will be racing around as soon as she comes home. She'll also outdo any baby in her ability to gnaw, dig, and cause general mayhem. The time to prepare is before you have a Cocker underfoot.

Most of us simply can't convert our homes to an entirely puppy-proof habitat. Instead, it is more practical to make part of your home off-limits to your dog, or to confine your dog in a relatively small area at first. That area should not be your garage, because for dogs it's one of the most danger-

ous rooms in the house. It also shouldn't be a bathroom, because bathrooms tend to be claustrophobic and also often contain pills and poisons. The kitchen can be a problem because your pup will be trying to trip you while you cook. You can use baby gates to partition off areas; this way your pup can still see you and so not feel shut away. Do not get the accordion type, which can catch the puppy's head and strangle her.

Another solution is to buy a small playpen for dogs, called an exercise pen (X-pen) and available from pet-supply catalogs, that you can place on a waterproof floor in a safe room that you're in a lot. You also need a crate, available from most pet-supply stores, which your pup can use as her private bedroom. If you place the crate in the exercise pen you can have a tiny safe indoor yard for your dog when you have to be out of the house.

Most show Cockers are trained to relieve themselves in an X-pen, especially the kind with a raised grid floor. This enables them to relieve themselves without getting their feet and coat messed up from the ground.

Cockers and Crates

Every Cocker should be crate trained. A crate-trained dog will be more comfortable if she must be crated when at the veterinarian's, while traveling, or at home recuperating from an illness. Crates make house-training much easier. A dog that is not crate trained may scream, bite at the crate, and rip up the bedding if you just plunk her in there and leave her.

A crate is neither a place of punishment nor a storage box for your dog. If you use it for either, your Cocker will come to dislike it. Teach your Cocker to like her crate by placing her in it when she begins to fall asleep. Keep the door open at first. During the day, give her treats in it, at first near the door, then gradually farther back in the crate. Give her a long-lasting treat or an interactive toy. Make sure that you build only good associations with the crate. Don't put your dog in the crate and then play with other dogs, eat, or do other things that simply make her think of the crate as barrier between her and fun. Most of all, don't overuse it.

Alone Time

Don't forget to accustom your puppy to being alone. Dogs are not naturally loners, and being alone is very stressful for them. Accustoming your Cocker to being by herself must be done gradually so she knows you're coming back soon. Save a special interactive chew toy to give her when you're leaving so she will have something to occupy her. Despite your efforts, many Cockers will develop separation anxiety. Seek professional help if your Cocker gets upset, pants, and destroys things when left alone.

Help with Housetraining

High on the list of a Cocker puppy's pleasures in life are peeing and pooping. High on your list of priorities is getting your puppy to do both outdoors. The problem is that emptying a full bladder or bowel feels good, so that every time your pup does it, she is rewarded. The more she does it in the wrong place, the more she builds a positive association with doing so, and the harder it is to teach her otherwise. In fact, puppies begin to make this association and to learn preferred elimination areas as early as five weeks of age. This is one reason it's important to get your puppy from a breeder who does not raise pups in cages or where they never get a chance to eliminate outdoors.

It's not only the reward aspect. The olfactory cues of your dog's own urine and feces scream out, "Here's your bathroom!" beckoning her to go on the rug again. This is why thorough cleaning with enzymatic dog cleaners is a vital part of housetraining.

You wouldn't expect to potty train a child by just plopping her on a toilet

Puppy Proofing 101

Fill in the following checklist:

Check all over for
- [ ] uncovered electrical outlets
- [ ] open stairways, decks, or balconies
- [ ] unsecured doors

Check the kitchen for
- [ ] open cabinets holding cleaners and degreasers
- [ ] accessible garbage pails holding enticing rancid food and splintering bones
- [ ] pan handles extending invitingly over stovetop edges
- [ ] plastic wraps, which can become lodged in the intestines

Check the dining room for
- [ ] hanging tablecloths, which if pulled, can bring dishes crashing down
- [ ] swinging doors, which can trap a puppy's head and neck

Check the family room for
- [ ] fireplace without a secure fire screen
- [ ] unsteady bookcases
- [ ] craft or sewing kits
- [ ] heavy statues or vases

Check the bedrooms for
- [ ] children's toys
- [ ] open closets, especially shoe closets

Check the bathrooms for
- [ ] pills and medicines
- [ ] hair treatments
- [ ] drain cleaners
- [ ] toilets with open lids
- [ ] razors
- [ ] diaper pails

Check the garage for
- [ ] antifreeze
- [ ] fuels, cleaners, paints—just about anything in a can
- [ ] batteries
- [ ] nails and screws
- [ ] herbicides, insecticides, and fertilizers
- [ ] rodent bait

Check the yard for
- [ ] weak fence
- [ ] rotted limbs
- [ ] unfenced pool
- [ ] cocoa mulch
- [ ] nut trees
- [ ] pointed sticks at eye level
- [ ] predators
- [ ] treated lawns
- [ ] poisonous plants
- [ ] insect hives

and walking away; don't expect to housebreak your puppy by shoving her out the door and walking away. If you do she'll huddle by the door until she can be reunited with you, and then will rush inside and pee or poop on the floor. Instead, no matter how rushed you are or how daunting the weather, go outside with her, and when she eliminates outside praise her and give her a treat just as you would reward her for any other trick

Put your stuff away! Puppies will teach you to either be a good housekeeper or accept losses with grace.

you might teach her. Don't wait until she's back inside; that's too late.

Young puppies have poor bladder and bowel control. A rule of thumb is that a puppy can hold itself for as many hours as the pup is months old. That means a two-month-old can wait for two hours, or a four-month-old for four hours, up to about six months old. Always take the puppy out before her regularly scheduled program of pee or poop. Also get her outside as soon as she awakens, soon after she eats, in the middle of playing, or any time you see her sniffing or circling.

But who can devote every moment to following a puppy? Not many people, which is why crates are such popular housetraining tools.

Puppies have an inborn desire to keep their den unsoiled, and that translates to the crate. If your puppy is in the crate, she'll learn to hold herself until you let her out, as long as you don't make unreasonable demands.

As your puppy gets better at controlling herself you can gradually enlarge her personal space. Start by placing her bed or crate in a tiny enclosed area—an area only a couple of feet beyond the boundary of her bed. Be especially vigilant so you can prevent her from soiling this area. Once she goes several days without soiling her area, make it just a little bit larger, and then larger again.

If you can't be home to take her out as often as she needs to go, con-

Carpet Cleaning

1. Pick and soak up as much of the deposit as possible.

2. Add a little water and again soak up as much as possible. If you have a rug cleaner that extracts liquid, now is the time to use it.

3. Apply an enzyme digester-type odor neutralizer (these are products specifically made for dog accidents); use enough to penetrate the pad. Leave it on for a long time, following directions.

4. Cover the area with plastic so it doesn't dry out before the digester can break down the urine.

5. Add a nice odor, such as a mixture of lavender oil or vanilla with baking soda, to the area.

6. Let it air out, then vacuum.

sider installing a doggy door that leads to a safe outdoor area. Enclose just enough indoor area so she can get from her crate to the door.

If you don't have a doggy-door option, you may have to resort to indoor plumbing. You can opt for the old newspaper standby, but be forewarned that soiled newspapers smell horrible. Better than paper are sod squares; after all, that's what you're trying to teach your puppy to use outside. When they're soiled, just plant them and look forward to a newly sodded yard by the time she's housebroken. Either way, start by covering the entire area and gradually reduce the size of coverage so the dog is aiming just for the paper or sod.

No matter how diligent you are, your Cocker will have accidents. If you catch her in the act, pick her up quickly and whisk her outside. If you don't see her doing it, there's nothing you can do. She was not being sneaky or spiteful, and she will have no idea what your problem is if you start yelling, pointing, and rubbing her nose in it. Such behavior will only convince her that every once in while, for no apparent reason, you go insane.

When will it ever end? It depends. A few gifted dogs are house-trained by three months of age, but five or six months is far more common. If your Cocker appears to urinate abnormally frequently, have your veterinarian check her for a urinary tract infection.

Smart Starts for Smart Spaniels

In terms of learning ability, an 8-week-old puppy's behavior and brain-wave activity function at nearly adult levels. In fact, a puppy's ability to learn slightly decreases beyond the age of 16 weeks. If you wait until your Cocker puppy is older for her first lessons, she is more likely to be confused and intimidated by this bizarre new game you've devised. Don't put off such an important part of life by assuming your pup is too young to learn. The things you teach her now, whether sit, stay, come, or stay off the furniture, will be second nature to her for the rest of her life.

Little puppies don't come with an instruction book telling them right from wrong. It's your job to guide them with understanding and clear signals.

These early months are also the time your Cocker will be learning about the world and her place in it. The lessons she learns now will shape her social life for years to come. Like all dogs, Cockers begin life relatively fearless, but gradually become more cautious with age. Eventually they become suspicious of novel situations and objects, adjusting to them with greater difficulty. This is why it's important to expose your pup to as much as possible while she's too young to be afraid; then when she meets the same experience later in life she will already know it's nothing to fear. That means exposing her to men, women, children, dogs, cats, traffic, stairs, noises, grooming, leash walking, crates, and even time spent by herself. Exposing doesn't mean overwhelming. A bad experience is worse than no experience. Good experiences are low stress and involve lots of rewards.

This race to expose your puppy to other places and experiences unfortunately presents a dilemma. Until your pup is at least 12 weeks old and has had two sets of puppy vaccinations, you should avoid exposing her to strange dogs or places lots of dogs frequent. However, you should still be able to find places where she can

Body language (clockwise from upper left): submissive, nervous, dominant, and playful positions.

meet people and experience new things without taking undue risks.

Meeting Children

Children are drawn to cute Cocker puppies, so be sure your pup isn't mobbed by a crowd of puppy petters. It's best to let your pup meet children one by one, with both child and pup on the ground. That way the pup can't be stepped on or dropped. Children must be taught that puppies can't be handled roughly. Dogs and young children should always be supervised for the well-being of both. Dogs and babies should also be supervised. Always make a fuss over the dog when the baby is around so the dog will associate the baby with good times.

Meeting Your Other Dog

If you already have a dog, he may not be as thrilled as you are about welcoming this little nuisance into his kingdom. The best way for your Cocker to make new canine friends is to introduce them on neutral territory, preferably by walking along together for a short distance. Since your puppy probably doesn't know how to walk on lead yet, that may not be possible. In that case, keep the older dog on lead but don't allow the pup to maul him. It may take a week or so for your other dog to warm up to this pesky intruder. Make sure your older dog always gets fed and

It's easier to learn about cats as a puppy, but it's never too late to make introductions as long as they're done in a controlled environment.

petted first, and let him know he is still number one with you. Lock the pup away if need be so your older dog gets special time with you. Feed him special treats when the puppy comes around so he will learn to associate the puppy with good times.

Your Cocker pup will naturally revere your older dog as a minor deity, and your older dog may have to give the youngster some warning growls or snaps to keep her out of his hair. Let him mildly reprimand her if she's out of hand, but try to remove her from him so it doesn't get to that point.

Meeting Your Cat

Introduce the family cat to your puppy in a similar way, except let them meet indoors where the cat can get out of the way. The cat is more likely to have the winning edge, so you may have to crate the pup at first for her own safety. Cockers and cats can become close friends, but it's mostly up to the cat!

Be consistent. If she gets on forbidden furniture, simply take her off and make sure you spend a lot of time on the floor with her. Also make sure she has some cuddly dog beds near where you will be sitting or sleeping. Cockers do like their creature comforts.

Leash Walking

Your Cocker will need a leash and either a collar or harness. Many people find a harness is easier for walking a Cocker than a collar because it has less chance of being pulled over the head. However, a harness encourages a dog to pull and can be difficult to use when training. If you use a collar, choose a buckle or martingale collar. A slip, or choke, collar is fine to use while walking your dog in public, but you must never leave it on when she's unsupervised. Your leash should be nylon or leather, never chain, because chain is difficult to handle. It also tends to smack your Cocker in the face.

The first time you put a harness or collar on your Cocker pup she may roll around and bite at it. Distract her with lots of treats or even a game. Have her wear it for only a short time and remove it while she's being good. Repeat several times a day until she associates a collar or harness with good times.

Now for the leash. Start by letting your puppy lead you around the

House Rules

Do you like your furniture? Would you jump up on your favorite chair and dance around on it with mud on your shoes? Would you take a razor blade to the arms and slice them up? If not, you may wish to keep your Cocker puppy off your furniture from the start.

You do have choices. Either let your puppy on the furniture, which is admittedly fun, and accept that you will suffer some damage, or keep your puppy off the furniture from the start. Don't let her up when she's young and then change your mind later. That's not fair.

Feed your puppy food made for puppies. Of course, she may have her own ideas.

house and yard. If she appears glued in place, pick her up and move her to another place, or entice her to take a few steps by luring her with a treat. Gradually lure her more and more; require that she take a few steps along with you before she gets the treats. Gradually she'll figure out that walking alongside you turns you into a human snack machine.

Puppy Care

Your Cocker youngster needs special care to grow into her potential. Start with a veterinary exam within a day of bringing her home. Your veterinarian is your best source of individualized health care, but you should be aware of the basics.

Puppy Meals

Feed your Cocker puppy a high-quality food made especially for puppies. A young puppy should be fed four times a day. Let her eat as much as she wants in about twenty minutes, then pick up the bowl. From about 4 to 6 months of age, you can feed her either three or four times a day. From 6 to 9 months of age, three times a day, and then gradually cut down to twice a day by the time she's 12 months old. You can add snacks, but don't let her get fat. If you see her packing on the baby fat, cut down the amount she eats per meal.

Vaccinations

In recent years veterinary institutions have revised their stance on vaccinations, adopting a more individualized approach for adults. However, the basic concepts of puppy vaccination remain the same. Without well-timed vaccinations your Cocker could be vulnerable to deadly communicable diseases.

Vaccinations are divided into core vaccines, which are advisable for all dogs, and noncore vaccines, which are advisable only for some dogs. Core vaccines are those for rabies,

Your puppy is vulnerable to a host of diseases and parasites at this young age. Don't put off protecting her.

distemper, parvovirus, and hepatitis (using the CAV-2 vaccine, not the CAV-1, which can cause adverse reactions and is still sold by some feed stores). Noncore vaccines include those for leptospirosis, corona virus, tracheobronchitis, Lyme disease, and giardia. Your veterinarian can advise you if your dog's lifestyle and environment put her at risk for these diseases. Most boarding kennels require a kennel cough vaccination within a year, as well as core vaccinations.

A puppy receives her early immunity through her dam's colostrum during the first few days of nursing. As long as she still has that, any vaccinations you give her won't provide sufficient immunity. But after several weeks, maternally derived immunity begins to fade. As it fades, both the chance of a vaccination's being

effective and the chance of getting a communicable disease rise. The problem is that immunity diminishes at different times in different dogs. So starting at around 6 weeks of age, a series of vaccinations are given to a puppy to catch the time when they will be effective while leaving as little unprotected time as possible. During this period of uncertainty it's best not to take your pup around places where unvaccinated dogs may congregate. Some deadly viruses, such as parvovirus, can remain in the soil for six months after an infected dog has shed the virus in its feces there.

A sample core vaccination protocol for puppies suggests giving a three-injection series at least two weeks apart, with each injection containing distemper (or measles for the first injection), parvovirus, adenovirus

2 (CAV-2), and parainfluenza (CPIV). The series should not end before 12 weeks of age. A booster is given one year later, and then every three years. Rabies should be given at 16 weeks of age, with boosters at one- to three-year intervals according to local law.

The topic of how frequently boosters should be given is currently under scrutiny. Some owners elect to test their dogs' blood titers (the amount of anitbodies found in the blood) to various diseases to see if a booster is needed. A high titer generally indicates protection, but a low titer doesn't mean the dog isn't protected.

Some proponents of natural rearing condemn vaccinations and refuse to use them. They use homeopathic nosodes instead, and point to the fact that their dogs don't get sick as proof that these remedies work. However, their dogs' good fortune is probably the result of herd immunity; that is, as long as most other dogs are vaccinated, homeopathically treated dogs probably never come in contact with the infectious agents. No controlled study has ever supported the effectiveness of nosodes. Vaccinations are not without a downside, but they are essential components of your dog's healthy future. Don't take chances.

Deworming

Your pup should have been checked and dewormed if necessary before coming home with you. Most pups have worms at some point because certain types of worms lie dormant and protected in the dam until hormonal changes caused by her pregnancy activate them and enable them to infect her puppies. Your pup can also pick up worms from the ground in places where dogs congregate. The best prevention at home is to clean up feces immediately. Some heartworm preventives also guard against many types of worms. Get your puppy regular fecal checks for worms, but don't deworm her unnecessarily. Avoid over-the-counter worm medications, which are neither as safe nor as effective as those available from your veterinarian.

If you see small, flat, white segments in your dog's stool, she may have tapeworms. Tapeworms are acquired when your pup eats a flea, so the best prevention is flea prevention. Special medication is required to get rid of tapeworms.

Heartworm Prevention

Heartworms can kill your dog. They are carried by mosquitoes, so if there is any chance of a single mosquito biting your Cocker, she needs to be on heartworm preventive medication. Ask your veterinarian when she should begin taking the medication, as it may vary according to your location. Dogs over 6 months of age should be checked for heartworms with a simple blood test before beginning a course of prevention. The once-a-month preventive is safe, convenient, and effective. Treatment is available for heartworms, but it's far cheaper, easier, and safer to prevent them.

The classic play-bow position signals "Let's play!" Take your puppy up on the invitation.

Spaying and Neutering

Before you start imagining the joy of breeding, think about the inconvenience of having an intact adult, the dangers of breeding, the work involved in caring for puppies, the expense incurred in raising them, the difficulty of finding good homes, and the lifelong responsibility it entails.

An intact (unspayed) female comes into estrus twice a year, usually beginning at around 8 months of age. Each heat period lasts for about three weeks, during which she will have a bloody discharge that will ruin your furnishings or necessitate her being crated for three weeks or wearing little britches (if you forget to remove them when you let her out to eliminate, your will have a real mess on your hands). Her scent, which she will exude by urinating as much as possible, will advertise your home as a roadside brothel, and you may have lots of uninvited canine Don Juans camping at your door. If you have an intact male of your own, he will drive you insane with his relentless panting, whining, shaking, and clawing. It will be the worst three weeks of your life.

How would you find homes for the pups? Do you trust that the people who answer your advertisements will give your pup a home as good as yours? Will you commit to being responsible for that pup's well-being for the rest of its life? Will you take every puppy back if their new owners should tire of them or otherwise not be able to keep them? That could add up to a houseful of Cockers!

Good Cocker breeders make these commitments, and more. They screen for hereditary defects, prove their dogs in some form of competition, educate themselves, and stand by their puppies for a lifetime. They often require that buyers neuter or spay their dogs because they know too well the problems dog breeding can create. They also recognize the health advantages that go along with spaying and neutering.

Spaying negates the possibility of pyometra, a potentially fatal infection of the uterus. Spaying before the first season significantly reduces the chance of breast cancer. Intact males are more likely to roam or fight, and to develop testicular cancer and prostatitis. The major drawbacks to spaying and neutering are that each procedure requires surgery and anesthesia, that many spayed and neutered dogs gain weight, and that some spayed females develop urinary incontinence. Talk to your veterinarian and breeder about the pros and cons.

Playtime

Don't be so preoccupied with the work of raising a puppy that you forget to have fun. It's just as important. Play is one of the reasons we have dogs; it cements the human-canine bond and, perhaps more importantly, gives us an excuse to act silly.

Play is an important component of learning. Few things can motivate as strongly as fun and games. Play provides a safe arena in which your puppy can learn new behaviors and self-control. It's an ideal situation in which to help an insecure puppy gain confidence or teach a puppy with

overly competitive tendencies to cooperate. Insecure dogs may need to start by playing cooperative games, such as learning fun tricks, playing fetch, searching for hidden treats, or playing alongside you with cat toys or other toys that are easily squeaked or manipulated. Searching and learning games are very good for pushy puppies.

Fetching is part of the Cocker's natural repertoire, so is usually a popular game. Just don't succumb to chasing her around after a toy. She needs to learn that if she doesn't bring you the ball, it means the game is over. Competitive games, such as tugging, should be used only if your dog has already been taught a release word. If she releases the toy on cue, she gets a treat in exchange. Most Cockers have soft mouths, meaning they don't grip or tug very hard. Otherwise that would spell disaster when retrieving a bird in the field!

"When are we going to play?"

Chapter Five
Cocker College

Your Cocker is one of the family, a member of the household. Like other members, he needs to follow the house rules. Cockers can learn these rules easily, but they do best if they are taught using positive reinforcement.

Some Cockers can be soft-natured, and some can be tough characters, but all do best when taught using reward-based training rather than punishment. Although they may succumb to forceful methods, such methods will seldom help you and your Cocker establish the partnership you may envision. Training a dog using these methods may not be what you were taught many years ago, but it's easy to learn. And your Cocker's good manners will be your reward.

Coaxing Your Cocker

Nobody likes being forced to comply, but everybody likes to be rewarded. You don't work for free; why should your Cocker? New training methods focus on rewards and positive associations. They produce happy, well-trained dogs that are eager to learn more. Traditional methods that rely on punishment are good only for teaching a dog to do nothing—and if you want a dog that does nothing, you should get a stuffed toy dog!

In the old days your dog had to wear a choke, or slip, collar for training. That's because training traditionally involved correcting the dog with a quick snap and release. It wasn't supposed to choke him, but it was supposed to be startling. With positive methods you can use such a collar, but you're just as well off using a buckle collar. You won't be tugging on it. You will want a six-foot leash (not chain!) and maybe a twenty-foot light line.

Before you get started, remember these tips:
• Train in a quiet place away from distractions. Only when your dog learns a skill very well should you gradually start practicing it in other places.
• Don't try to train your dog if he's tired, hot, or has just eaten. You want him peppy and hungry for your fun and treats.

• Don't train your dog if you're impatient or mad. You won't be able to hide your frustration, and your dog will be uneasy.

• Keep your training sessions very short. Dogs learn best in ten- to fifteen-minute sessions. Always quit while he's still having fun and doing something he can do well. You can train him several times a day if you want.

Clickers and Cockers

You may have heard dog trainers talk about clicker training. It's a type of training that works very well with most animals, including dogs. Your Cocker learns to tune out a lot of what you say because it doesn't affect him. That means your voice is not always the best signal to use if you want to get his attention. Instead, something that makes a distinctive sound works much better for signaling "good!" By following the click sound with a reward, your dog quickly learns that the click means good. Because the click is faster and shorter than your voice, it can more precisely mark the moment your dog is doing something right. Clickers are inexpensive and available at pet stores, but you can use anything that makes a distinctive click sound.

Be sure to click immediately when your dog does what you want; it marks the behavior and tells the dog "Yes, that's it!" Then reward him as soon as you can after the click. And don't forget the praise! The click tells the dog he has done the right thing as he is learning something; after he knows how to do it, you can phase out the click, but not the praise and rewards. The click also tells the dog he can end the behavior, so once you click, don't expect your dog to continue sitting or doing whatever you've been teaching him.

No dog learns to do something perfectly at first. You have to teach him gradually, shaping his behavior closer and closer to what you want. By following the clicker sound with a reward, your dog tries to repeat what he did to get the click.

Here's how to teach your Cocker, whom we have imaginatively named "Cocky," to sit using clicker training. If you don't have a clicker, you can make a clicking sound or just say "Good!" each time the instructions tell you to click.

First, you'll need many, many tiny treats, such as small bits of hot dog. Then review these clicker basics:

• Always train in gradual steps. Give rewards for getting closer and closer to the final trick.

• Give a click instantly when your dog does what you want. The faster you click, the easier it is for your dog to figure out what you like.

• Give a reward as soon as you can after the click.

• Don't forget to praise and pet your dog as part of the reward!

• Say your dog's name just before you give the command so he knows the next word you babble is directed at him.

Well-trained dogs make gracious guests.

• Give the command just before you get the dog to do the behavior, not during or after it.

• Say a cue word (command) just once. Repeating it over and over won't help your dog learn it.

• Once your dog has learned the completed action and is doing it con-sistently, you don't have to click your approval any more. But you still need to praise and reward him.

Sit

The old way of teaching the *sit* was to pull up on your dog's collar and push down on his rear as you said *"Sit."* Training this first behavior using the clicker technique takes a little longer initially, but it lays the groundwork for faster learning in the long run.

You could go to a quiet room and wait for Cocky to *sit* on his own, and then click and reward him. That might take a while, but you could do it gradually. Wait for him to bend his knees and then click and reward, reinforcing him for squatting just a bit. Once he has learned to do that, you could wait until he squats a bit more before clicking, until finally, going in gradual steps, you would require him to actually *sit* before you click and reward. This method, too, can be time-consuming.

You can hasten the process by luring your dog into a sitting position. With his rear in a corner so he can't back up, take your treat and hold It just above and behind his nose, so he has to bend his rear legs to look up at it. Click and reward. Repeat several times, then move the treat farther back so he has to bend his legs more. Keep on until he has to *sit.*

Only when he is sitting reliably when you lure him do you introduce the cue word: *"Cocky, sit."* Gradually fade out luring with the treat so you are using just your empty hand, and eventually, nothing. Be sure to continue rewarding him afterward, though.

Now you've taught your Cocker to *sit* without jerking on his collar or pushing on his rear. He probably thinks this is pretty fun. He probably would like to learn some other ways

Use a treat to lure your dog's nose up, head back, and rear down into a sit.

to con you out of some good treats. Now's your chance to teach him.

Stay

What's the use of teaching your dog to *sit* if he only touches his rear to the ground and then jumps back up? Technically, you don't need to teach your dog a separate *stay* command, because he should remain in position until he gets the click from you. The click ends the behavior. Realistically, it is easier to teach your dog a cue to *stay.* Otherwise he may think that you are waiting for him to try a new behavior, and may attempt one at the least opportune moment.

Because staying is essentially asking the dog to do nothing, we teach it in a different way than we would most other behaviors. For starters, we introduce the cue word as soon as we start teaching the dog to *stay.* That's because your dog otherwise would not know the difference between a *sit* where you forgot to reward him and this new behavior of not moving. Second, we don't use a clicker. That's because staying is an imprecise behavior that relies on duration, not action. In addition, because the clicker signals the end of the behavior, the dog would be free to get up for his reward, thus creating a situation where you are rewarding the dog for getting up.

1. With your dog sitting, say *"Stay"* and hold your palm in a *stop* signal in front of his face. Wait for a few seconds, then reward him and say *"OK!"*

2. If your dog is having a problem getting the concept, you can have him *sit* on a raised surface or behind a small barrier so it's more difficult for him to come to you.

3. Work up gradually to a longer duration. If he gets up, simply put him back in position and start over, decreasing the duration you expect of him.

Lure your dog's nose downward between the front legs until he's lying down.

4. Next, work on moving to different positions around your dog, still remaining close to him. Move in front, to either side, and behind your dog. Then move farther away from him.

5. Either click or use a release word, such as *"OK!"* to tell the dog he can get up.

Down

Having a dog that will lie down quietly is a big help when you want him to stay in the room and impress your guests, if you take him to an outdoor café that allows dogs, or anytime you need him to stay out of the way. Here's one way to teach it:

1. With your dog sitting, show him a treat and move the treat toward the ground. This often works better if your dog is on a raised surface so you can move the treat below the level of that surface. You may need to place your other hand gently on his shoulders to prevent him from jumping up.

2. If his elbows touch the ground, click and reward him. Even if he goes only partway, click and reward just for lowering a bit. Then repeat, clicking and rewarding for going down a little more and a little more.

3. Next, repeat but without a treat in the hand you have been using to lure him. Gradually abbreviate your hand movements until you are using only a small hand signal.

4. Add the verbal cue *"Down"* right before the hand signal.

5. Practice the *down-stay* just as you did the *sit-stay.*

It's often easier to teach stationary exercises on a raised surface.

Come

Coming when called is the single most important behavior your Cocker can learn. The best time to start is when he is still a puppy, and the best method is with lots of treats and play. A great way to teach your puppy to *come* is with the help of a friend and the use of a long hallway or other enclosed area.

1. Have your helper hold your dog while you back away, showing your dog a treat or toy. Once the dog is pulling to get to you and the reward, the helper should release him so he can run to you. You can even turn and run away to increase your pup's enthusiasm. Mark the moment he touches you, then quickly reward him.

2. Eventually you want to be able to touch his collar so you don't end up with a dog that dances around just outside your reach. To do that, wait until you touch or hold his collar before marking and rewarding him.

3. Once he is running to you reli ably, add the cue *"Come!"* just before your helper releases him. Practice this several times for many sessions.

4. Once he is coming on cue, let him meander around on his own. Call *"Come"* and mark and reward him when he lets you touch his collar.

5. Finally, practice in lots of different places, gradually choosing areas with more distractions. Keep your dog on a long light line for his safety.

Always make coming to you rewarding. If you want your dog to come so you can give him a bath or put him to bed or do anything else he doesn't really like, go get him rather than call him. Practice calling him to you during walks, giving him a reward, then letting him run free again.

Heel

Most of the time you'll be content to have your dog walk alongside without pulling your arm out of joint. Sometimes, however, you may be in a crowded place and want him in a more precise position, such as the *heel* position. You can teach your dog how to *heel* by luring him. Because you would have to bend over to do this, you can use a stick and smear some peanut butter or other sticky treat on the end of it.

1. Lure your dog into *heel* position. That's on your left side, next to you but not crowding you, with his neck about even with your leg. Once there, click and reward him. You may not be able to get him there at first, so click and reward at first just for getting anywhere close. Then gradually reward him for getting closer and closer.

2. As he catches on, make the reward lure smaller and smaller,

Proper **heel** *position is at your left side, with neck roughly alongside your leg.*

instead giving him most of his reward from your other hand.

3. Next add the cue: *"Heel!"*

4. After he is heeling while you walk calmly, make staying in *heel* position a challenge by running and turning, clicking and rewarding when he is able to stick to your side. He'll think it's a fun game!

Cockers Behaving Badly

There's more to training than learning a few obedience exercises. The best-trained obedience dog can still be a nuisance to visitors and around the house unless you use your training know-how to prevent and cure behavior problems.

Jumping Up

This is a Cocker favorite. After all, your Cocker is probably convinced that any company has come to see him. Traditional training advice is to knee the dog in the chest or to step on his rear toes when he jumps up. These methods are potentially injurious to the dog, still rewarding because he remains the center of attention, and fail to give the dog a correct alternative behavior. The alternative has often been to simply lock the dog up when company arrives. This prevents the behavior that day, but tends only to make him more frenzied to jump up on a visitor the next time.

Instead, teach the dog to *sit* and *stay* instead of jumping up. Reward

By always associating coming to you with good things, your Cocker should race to you when called.

him with attention, kneeling beside him for greeting. If he jumps up, ignore him. He will eventually learn that the best way to get your attention, or your company's attention, is by doing as you ask, not by demanding it.

Stop It!

Is your Cocker always nudging you, barking at you, leaning on you, mouthing you, scratching doors, or stealing objects? These may be his attempts to get your attention. Most people react by attending to the dog, whether with an idle pat, an admonishment to stop it, a shove away, or even punishment. Unfortunately, even punishment is often better than nothing for dogs seeking attention, so their behavior is reinforced.

Because these dogs crave attention, you need to make sure they get it at regularly scheduled times that *you* choose, not the dog. Use this predictable time to train, play with, groom, or massage your dog, making him the focus of attention.

When the dog initiates any of these attention-seeking behaviors, he should be ignored. He must instead learn acceptable behaviors to earn your attention. Have him sit and stay. If he is generally unruly and wants to play, wait for him to be calm before you suggest going to play. This can be difficult because most owners are so relieved that the dog is finally quiet they don't want to get him riled up again. But if you wish to reward your excitable dog for being calm, you must acknowledge that you don't want a dog that never does anything. You want a dog that does things on *your* schedule.

Many behavior problems can be solved simply by paying attention to your dog and making sure he gets plenty of both physical and mental exercise.

Calm Down!

That Cocker wiggle is a familiar sight, starting at the tip of his tail and wagging its way to envelop the rest of his body. Cockers are happy, active dogs. Isn't that what you wanted? Yes and no. It would be nice if he would calm down sometimes!

Chances are your dog may be overactive for the amount of exercise you provide him. Remember, Cocker Spaniels were developed to hunt, running and sniffing for hours at a time. It's likely that your Cocker needs more exercise, both mental and physical. Jogging, games, and exercise can tire your dog physically, which is half the battle. Canine sports such as agility and flyball combine mental challenges with physical ones. Tracking is also a

good outlet, and hunting is one of the best ways to fulfill his needs.

Don't expect your dog to be calm without first working off some of his energy, but even then, he needs to be rewarded for calm behavior. Speak calmly and quietly. Ignore his pushy or overactive behavior. Reward him for sitting or lying down and staying, and for being calm as you gently pet and massage him. Maybe he just needs to learn how good relaxing can feel.

Give!

Cockers were bred to return downed birds to hand, but even a Cocker has a hard time resisting a good game of keep away, especially when you join in so willingly as he grabs your shoe and takes off into the yard. Each time you chase your dog with a toy or forbidden object, it rewards him because it is fun and he usually wins.

If you really want this behavior to stop, you have to stop chasing him—or at least set up some rules so he knows when the game is over.

Here is a way to teach a playfully possessive dog to relinquish objects on command:

1. Start with an old toy the dog doesn't care much about. Place it near the dog, pick it up, return it, and reward the dog for remaining calmly in place.

2. Replace the object with gradually more enticing ones, repeating the procedure. Remember to always praise and reward him with something worth getting.

3. When he is staying calmly and reliably, add a cue word: *"Give!"*

4. If he picks up the object, which he probably will eventually as it becomes more interesting, give the cue *"Give!"* and reward him for letting you take it.

5. If he does not give up the object, don't fight him for it. Just leave the room and ignore him. Game over.

Hush!

Cockers like to bark. Most Cocker owners like to hear them, but only once in a while. Dogs bark for different reasons, and understanding why your dog is barking is the first step to silencing him.

Some dogs bark because they are distressed, bored, or lonely. The best remedy is to bring them inside so they can share daily activities with the rest of the family. Isolated dogs are especially prone to barking nonstop. Give him something to do that's more fun than barking. It's hard to bark when you're busy chewing a bone or working the food out of a treat toy. And make sure he has plenty of exercise. It's hard to bark when you're asleep.

Other dogs bark because they are excited. You need to teach an excited dog that being quiet is more rewarding than barking. Wait until he is quiet for a moment and then give him a treat. This may be easier if you have him *sit* and *stay* first. Keep repeating this, gradually increasing how long he must be quiet before getting a treat. Add a cue word, such as *"Hush!"* as you start your timing. Eventually he learns that *"Hush!"* means that if he is quiet he will get a treat.

Don't yell at your dog to make him stop barking. He'll only think you are joining in the fun. Be calm and quiet yourself. If need be you can throw a noisy can on the ground to stop him briefly so he can be quiet enough to begin training.

Escaping

Some misbehavior is better prevented than treated, and the best prevention is often a strong fence or leash. Some Cockers are homebodies, while others want to roam and hunt. Make sure your fence is secure from the start so you don't inadvertently teach your dog how to solve fence puzzles and escape from your yard.

Hidden electric fences are seldom the best choice. Determined dogs can grit their teeth and run through, but are seldom as motivated to come back that way. Children, dognappers, and stray dogs can come into your yard and be bitten by, steal, or harass your dog.

Just because your dog has a big fenced yard doesn't mean you don't have to exercise and interact with him. Many dogs won't exercise in their own yard, and no yard can provide the human interaction your dog craves. Besides, you need the exercise!

Digging

Dogs dig. They dig because they are in pursuit of underground animals such as moles they can hear and smell, they dig to find a warm place or a cool place to rest, they dig to escape, they dig to bury and excavate treasures, and they dig for fun. You need to know why your dog digs so you can thwart him.

If he digs in long trenches along mole tunnels, he is in hot pursuit and your best bet is to keep moles out of your yard. Or just accept it! If he lies in his holes, he may be seeking protection from the elements. If he's hot, get him a child's wading pool. If he's cold, get him a warm shelter. If he is digging under a fence, bury wire mesh underground for several feet, going as deep as possible or bending toward the inside of the yard. If he is burying and digging up bones and treats, or if he is digging just for fun, get him his own sandbox. Salt it with bones, toys, and other fun things for him to find. Gradually bury them deeper and deeper so the game is more challenging. Make sure he is never rewarded by unearthing something outside the box.

Eating Feces

Many a dog owner has been appalled as their darling comes to lick them in the face with feces breath. What would possess such a nice dog to eat his own poop? Nobody knows, but it doesn't seem to be a nutritional deficiency or digestive disorder. It appears that eating feces may be a natural behavior for dogs, perhaps left over from their days as village

Even the best behaved Cockers may not always be perfect. But then, who is?

waste scavengers. Why some dogs do it and others don't is a mystery. Stopping it is a challenge.

The best cure and prevention is diligent feces removal. Adding hot sauce to the feces may deter some dogs, but others just gobble it down and run for the water bowl. Commercially available food additives, usually containing monosodium glutamate, can make the feces taste bad—or at least worse—and will dissuade some dogs. Some dogs must wear a muzzle to stop the behavior, but that can be messy when they still try. Finally, in some cases the dogs appear to exhibit a compulsion to eat feces; these dogs may be helped by drugs used to treat obsessive-compulsive behavior. Your veterinarian may be able to help.

Don't Fret the Small Stuff

You Cocker Spaniel is a dog, not a child in a fur suit. As such, he is going to do a lot of naturally doggy things that you won't like and can't stop. If your dog wants to roll in feces or carrion, it's easier to wash him off afterward or keep him on leash than it is to fruitlessly try to stop him. If he wants to eat cat feces, horse droppings, or other such delicacies, training is not going to dissuade him. As much as we advocate training your dog to behave himself, sometimes it's just easier on everyone if you remove temptation, roll with the punches, and worry about the big stuff. We prevent the bad behaviors we can, change the ones we must, accept the ones we're left with, and love him just the same.

Chapter Six

The Cocker Cookbook

Few areas of dog care are wrought with as much controversy as that of choosing the best diet for your dog. Given a choice, your Cocker would contend the best diet is whatever is on your plate. However, your job is to make an informed decision so you can provide your dog with a diet that is both tempting and nutritious.

Cocker Nutrition

Your Cocker Spaniel is a dog, and dogs are in the order Carnivora, but don't let that fool you into thinking he can eat only meat. True, meat makes up a large part of a healthy dog's diet, but dogs are technically omnivores, meaning they need a variety of foods in their diet. It's no secret that dogs like meat; it's also healthful for them and, because meat is highly digestible, means less stool volume for you to clean up and fewer gas problems for you to explain to your visitors.

How much meat? First, don't be deceived by names of commercial foods. Something that is labeled "beef flavored," for example, may not even contain beef, as long as feeding trials show that a dog recognizes it as beef. A food labeled "with beef" may contain as little as 3 percent beef. A beef "dinner" or "entrée" need not contain beef as its major ingredient, but beef products must make up at least 10 percent of the total product. Only a product in which beef makes up at least 70 percent of the total content can be labeled simply "beef" without any fancy modifiers.

Even if you don't bother to look at the ingredient list or the nutritional analysis of foods you eat, you need to do so for what your dog eats. Your dog's diet is a lot less varied than yours, and that means his health is much more dependent on the one or two types of food you feed him.

Commercial foods come in dry, canned, and moist varieties. Dry dog foods are generally the most healthful, provide needed chewing action, and are most economical, but tend to be less appealing. Many people mix dried foods with tastier canned foods, which are usually higher in fat. Semimoist foods are high in sugar and, although handy for travel, lack the better attributes of the other types of dog food.

Before you can compare percentages of nutrients, you have to consider that the varying moisture contents will affect your results. You can negate this difference by equating the food's dry matter, which you do by subtracting the listed moisture content. The remaining percentage is the food's dry matter, which you then use to divide into each listed nutrient percentage. For example, for a canned food that lists its moisture content as 75 percent and protein percentage as 10 percent, you would divide 10 percent by 25 percent and find the canned food contained 40 percent protein on a dry-matter basis.

Which nutrients should you be concerned about? The answer, of course, is all of them. Fortunately, dog food companies have done this for you. It still doesn't hurt to be familiar with some important concepts, however.

Protein provides the building blocks for bone, muscle, coat, and antibodies. Eggs, followed by meats, have higher-quality and more digestible proteins than do plant-derived proteins.

Fat provides energy and aids in the transport of vitamins. Too little fat in the diet (less than 5 percent dry matter) results in dry coats and scaly skin. Too much fat can cause diarrhea, obesity, and a reduced appetite for more nutritious foods. A recent study found that dog foods containing oil or fat among their first four ingredients were associated with a significantly higher rate of gastric torsion (bloat) in dogs that ate them.

Cockers, like all dogs, need more than just meat in their diets.

Carbohydrates abound in plant and grain ingredients. Dogs can't utilize their nutrients from carbohydrates unless the carbohydrates are cooked; even then, they use them to different degrees depending on their source. Carbohydrates from rice are best, followed by potato and corn, and then wheat, oats, and beans. Excessive carbohydrates in the diet can cause diarrhea, flatulence, and poor athletic performance.

Vitamins are essential for normal life functions. Dogs require the following vitamins in their diet: A, D, E, B1, B2, B12, niacin, pyridoxine, pantothenic acid, folic acid, and choline. Most dog foods have these vitamins

Water is the most essential nutrient. Keep a bowl of fresh water available at all times.

feeling, although its effectiveness is controversial. Too much fiber causes large stool volume and can impair the digestion of other nutrients.

Water is essential for life. It dissolves and transports other nutrients, helps regulate body temperature, and helps lubricate joints. Dehydration can cause or complicate many health problems. Keep a bowl of clean, cool water available for your Cocker at all times.

How much of each nutrient your dog needs depends on its life stage, activity level, and health. Growing dogs need more protein, active dogs need more protein and fat, fat dogs need more protein and less fat, and sick dogs need a reduction or addition of various ingredients according to their illnesses.

added in their optimal percentages, so that supplementing with vitamin tablets is rarely necessary.

Minerals help build tissues and organs, and are part of many body fluids and enzymes. Deficiencies or excesses can cause anemia, poor growth, strange appetite, fractures, convulsions, vomiting, weakness, heart problems, and many other disorders. Again, most commercial dog foods have minerals added in their ideal percentages. It is not a good idea to supplement your dog's diet with minerals, especially calcium.

Fiber, such as beet pulp or rice bran, should make up a small part of the dog's diet. It's often used in weight-loss diets to give the dog a full

Cockers, Taurine, and Cardiomyopathy

Some cockers have a heart condition that may be affected by levels of taurine—and perhaps carnitine—in the diet. Taurine is an amino acid most readily obtained from fish, meat, eggs, and dairy products. However, most dogs do not need to ingest taurine to maintain adequate levels in their blood plasma. For some reason, though, some Cocker Spaniels with a serious disease of the heart muscle called dilated cardiomyopathy are also deficient in taurine. Supplementing these dogs

What's That Ingredient?

Here's how to decipher the list of ingredients in commercial dog food:

• *Meat:* mammal flesh, including muscle, skin, heart, esophagus, and tongue.

• *Meat by-products:* cleaned mammal organs including kidneys, stomach, intestines, brain, spleen, lungs, and liver, plus blood, bone, and fatty tissue.

• *Meat meal and bonemeal:* product rendered from processed meat and meat products.

• *Poultry by-products:* cleaned poultry organs, plus feet and heads.

• *Poultry by-products meal:* product rendered from processed poultry by-products.

• *Fish meal:* dried ground fish.

• *Beef tallow:* fat.

• *Soybean meal:* by-product of soybean oil.

• *Cornmeal:* ground whole corn kernels.

• *Corn gluten meal:* dried residue after the removal of bran, germ, and starch from corn.

• *Brewer's rice:* fragmented rice kernels separated from milled rice.

• *Cereal food fines:* small particles of human breakfast cereals.

• *Beet pulp:* dried residue from sugar beets, added for fiber.

• *Peanut hulls:* ground peanut shells, added for fiber.

• *BHA, BHT, ethoxyquin, sodium nitrate, tocopherols (vitamins C and E):* preservatives. Of these, the tocopherols are generally considered to present the fewest health risks, but they also have the shortest shelf life.

with taurine along with carnitine, an amine made from certain other amino acids and available from red meat, raises the taurine levels to normal and, while it does not totally cure the heart, allows the dogs to maintain a normal quality of life. This is discussed more on page 60 in the health chapter.

What does this mean for the average Cocker Spaniel owner? First, cardiomyopathy is uncommon in Cocker Spaniels, so you don't need to rush out and buy your dog a side of beef. You do, however, need to make sure your dog is getting some source of taurine-rich food or supplement. Some people who have tried feeding their dogs vegetarian diets have found they have taurine-deficient dogs with cardiomyopathy. It's just not a good idea with Cockers.

Cocker Coats and Diet

Healthy skin depends on good nutrition. Although rare, some Cockers suffer from a condition called Vitamin A-responsive dermatosis. Vitamin A, which is found most abun-

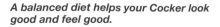
A balanced diet helps your Cocker look good and feel good.

dantly in liver, is essential in the keratinization process, which is important for skin cell growth and turnover. Both too high and too low levels of vitamin A can give rise to seborrhea-like signs, with scaling, greasy skin, hair loss, itching, and small eruptions on the skin.

Vitamin A-responsive dermatosis is a rare condition that is seen almost exclusively in Cocker Spaniels even when they are fed an apparently nutritionally adequate diet. A Cocker Spaniel with seborrhea that doesn't respond to standard treatments should be evaluated for the possibility of vitamin A deficiency, and possibly given vitamin A supplements, However, because too much vitamin A is just as bad as too little, this should be done only under a veterinarian's advice.

Special Diets

Specially formulated diets can greatly add to a sick dog's quantity and quality of life. Unfortunately, dogs often grow tired of them quickly. By understanding what ingredients must be avoided in a particular illness, you may be able to include some treats in the diet as well.

Food allergies: Studies have suggested that Cockers are prone to developing food allergies in which the immune system reacts to particular proteins. Beef and corn are common culprits. By feeding a bland diet of proteins the dog has never eaten, such as venison, duck, or rabbit, the allergic symptoms (which range from diarrhea to itchiness) should subside. If they do, ingredients are added back one by one until an ingredient is found that triggers the response. You may have to keep your dog on a diet of novel proteins forever—at least until he develops an allergy to it and you must move to another novel protein. Some hypoallergenic diets consist not of novel proteins, but of protein molecules that are too small to cause allergic reactions.

Urinary stones: Dogs that tend to form urinary stones may be helped by diets high in certain minerals. Such diets are also usually high in fiber. Because there are several types of urinary stones, your veterinarian can suggest which diet is appropriate.

Diabetes mellitus: Diabetic dogs need diets high in complex carbohydrates, and they need to be fed on a strict schedule.

Liver disease: Dogs with liver disease must eat to get better, but they should avoid meat and instead get their protein from milk (unless it causes diarrhea) or soy products. They need small meals of complex carbohydrates frequently throughout the day. Vitamin A and copper levels must be kept low.

Pancreatitis: Pancreatitis is often precipitated by a high-fat meal, especially in older, fatter dogs. Dogs with pancreatitis need to be fed a low-fat diet to lessen the likelihood of recurrence.

Congestive heart failure: Dogs with heart failure require a low-sodium diet (balanced with potassium) in order to lower their blood pressure. This will help reduce the accumulation of fluid in the lungs or abdomen. Cockers with cardiomyopathy should be screened for taurine deficiency and supplemented with taurine or fed taurine-rich foods.

Kidney disease: Diets for kidney disease should have moderate quantities of high-quality protein. Proteins produce toxic wastes that impaired kidneys cannot clear, causing the dog to feel ill. Feeding him higher-quality protein, such as eggs (especially egg whites), beef, or chicken, produces the fewest toxic by-products in comparison to protein used. Lower levels of high-quality protein will make the dog feel better in advanced kidney failure. Controlling phospho-rus, common in meats and cheeses, is an essential part of diet management. Sodium must also be kept low. Feeding a high-fat diet will add essential calories.

Prescription diets are available through your veterinarian for all these conditions. In addition, your veterinarian can give you recipes for home-prepared diets that meet these requirements.

Home-Prepared Diets

Many people seek alternatives to commercial foods, feeling they are not a natural way to feed dogs and that dogs do better when fed fresh, whole foods with top-quality ingredients. Although these points are true, it is extremely difficult to design a balanced diet on your own.

If they are prepared according to recipes devised by certified canine nutritionists, home-prepared diets should have the correct proportion of nutrients. Unlike commercial dog foods, such diets are not customarily tested on generations of dogs, which makes them vulnerable to looking healthy on paper but not being properly digested or utilized. They can also be labor-intensive, although large batches can be made and frozen.

Some people prefer to feed their dogs a BARF (Bones And Raw Food) diet, with the idea that such a diet better emulates that of a wild dog. They feed raw, meaty bones along with vegetables. Although dogs have better resistance to bacterial food poisoning than humans do, such diets have nonetheless occasionally been associated with food poisoning, often from salmonella. Commercially available meats may be awash in contaminated liquids. Perhaps the worst problem with BARF diets, however, is that most people who claim to use them never bother to establish nutritional balance, but instead rely on friends who may advocate a solid regimen of chicken wings or some equally unbalanced diet.

What about table scraps? Although too many table scraps can throw off the nutrient balance, recent research has found that dogs that eat table scraps in addition to their regular commercial diet have less incidence of gastric torsion ("bloat"). But choose your scraps carefully. Avoid hunks of fat, which can bring on pancreatitis in susceptible dogs, and avoid the following human foods, which can be toxic to dogs:

• Onions cause a condition in which the red blood cells are destroyed. Eating an entire onion could be fatal.

• Chocolate contains theobromine, which can cause death in dogs.

• Macadamia nuts cause some dogs to get very ill; the cause isn't understood.

• Raisins and grapes have been associated with kidney failure and extreme sudden toxicity in some dogs.

• Sugar-free candy and gum containing the artificial sweetener xylitol has been implicated in several cases of toxicity in some dogs that have eaten large amounts of it. It appeared to cause a sudden drop in blood sugar in these dogs.

Weight Problems

Gauge how much to feed your Cocker by how much he eats and how much he weighs. Growing pups need a lot of food, and unless they're getting porky, they should be allowed to eat what they want. But if they continue eating the same amounts, they risk getting overweight.

All dogs metabolize food at different rates, so nobody can tell you just how much to feed your dog. Your job is to monitor your dog's weight and adjust his food and exercise accordingly. You should be able to feel (but not see) the ribs slightly when you run your hands along the ribcage. An indication of a waistline should be visible both from above and from the side. There should be no dimple in front of the tail or fat roll on the withers.

Some disorders, such as heart disease, Cushing's disease, hypothyroidism, or the early stages of diabetes, can cause a dog to appear fat. A dog in which only the abdomen is enlarged is especially suspect and should be examined by a veterinarian. A bloated belly in a puppy may signal internal parasites.

Most fat-looking Cockers are fat because they simply eat more calories than they burn. They need to lose weight, which you can achieve by feeding smaller portions of a lower-calorie food. Commercially available diet foods supply about 15 percent fewer calories compared to standard foods. Protein levels should remain moderate to high to avoid muscle loss when dieting. It's hard to resist those pleading eyes when your Cocker begs for a treat, but treats add up to lots of calories during the day. Substitute fattening treats with carrot sticks or rice cakes. Keep him away from where you prepare or eat human meals, and instead of feeding him leftovers when you're through eating, make it a habit to go for a walk. It will do you both good!

Dog food labels don't include information on calories, so you may need to calculate them yourself. Proteins and carbohydrates both have about 3.5 calories per gram, and fat has about 8.5 calories per gram. By multiplying 3.5 times the percentage of protein and carbohydrates listed in the analysis, and 8.5 times the percentage of fat, and then adding these products together, you will have the total number of calories per gram of a food.

Although thin Cockers are rare compared to fat ones, they do exist. A thin Cocker should be checked by your veterinarian. Unexplained weight loss can be caused by heart disease, cancer, and any number of endocrine problems. If your dog checks out normal, you may be able to change his diet to improve his weight. Feed more meals of a higher-calorie food. Add canned food, ground beef, or a small amount of

Cockers are notorious when it comes to licking their bowl clean. But watch out—they are also prone to putting on too much weight.

chicken fat. Heating the food will often increase its appeal. Add a late-night snack; many dogs seem to have their best appetites late at night.

Remember, two of your Cocker's favorite things are eating and exercising. Increasing exercise is a good way to help keep the weight where it should be!

Changing Diets

If you change from one food to another, do it gradually over several days. Otherwise, your dog could get an upset stomach.

Chapter Seven
The Cocker Coiffure

Whether adorned in crowning glory or shorn in a sporty clip, a clean and groomed Cocker, with short nails and sparkling teeth, feels good about herself. She's a pleasure to caress, cuddle, and behold. Keeping her that way is part of the deal you made when choosing a Cocker Spaniel. It's a deal that both of you will enjoy keeping.

Your Cocker Spaniel sports a coat of awe-inspiring beauty—as long as you help her keep it that way. Cocker coat care requires dedication and know-how. Fortunately, you have choices.

You may have fallen in love with the opulent coat of the Cocker show dog. Be forewarned that maintaining such a coat is not a casual undertaking. You may be happier to compromise with a more moderate coat length, or even opt for a cute but handy short style.

Remember that a long coat needs daily care. If it gets wet, you must dry it. If it gets leaves and twigs in it, you must remove them. If it gets food, urine, or feces in it, you must wash them out. If you plan outdoor activities with your Cocker, you'll almost certainly be happier with a shorter coat.

All but the shortest styles still require regular brushing and bathing.

Professional Grooming

Most Cocker owners prefer to have their dogs professionally groomed. Groomers can be found in several places. Some have grooming shops, some have a grooming area in a veterinary office, some work from pet supply stores, some work from home, and some have mobile grooming vans that come to your front door. You still need to do some maintenance grooming at home, but by arranging a standard grooming appointment your Cocker's hair should never get out of hand. You should have your Cocker professionally groomed at least once every eight weeks.

The groomer will discuss various options for trims that best fit your lifestyle. He or she will also examine your dog to see if she's heavily matted. If she is, the cost of the grooming session will need to be higher to compensate for the greater amount of work involved in dematting. The

groomer may suggest that you have the dog clipped down, which will save time, money, and trauma to the dog. Only an experienced groomer should clip a matted dog because mats that reach the skin can be tricky to remove without causing damage. In fact, you may have to sign an acknowledgment that the groomer has informed you that the damaged skin may itch, peel, or form a rash.

The groomer will trim the nails, clean the ears, brush out the coat, remove any mats, and bathe the dog. During the bath, the groomer may empty the anal sacs. After the shampoo and cream rinse, the dog is blow-dried and brushed again. Then the dog is clipped and trimmed. The average time for a professional groomer to spend on a Cocker Spaniel is two and a half hours.

One of several advantages of having an experienced groomer work on your dog is that he or she may spot an abnormality that you would overlook. Infected anal sacs, skin disease, parasites, dental problems, and eye or ear problems are all often first noticed by alert groomers. Professional groomers are trained to handle dogs, even old and lame ones, safely and comfortably, but you should always advise them if your dog has special concerns. Professional groomers do not use drugs to sedate your dog for grooming, although they may use a muzzle in some cases.

Evaluating Groomers

Ask any prospective groomer for a tour of the facilities. It doesn't have to be fancy, but each dog should be in a clean cage or run, separated from the other dogs. Cages should be sanitized between dogs. Clipper and scissor blades should be cleaned with a sterilizing solution between dogs. Otherwise they can transfer bacteria and even parasites from one dog to another.

No dog should be left unsupervised on a grooming table, in a tub, or inside a closed cage with a dryer aimed at it. A dog on a grooming table may be held there by a groom-

Trimming a Cocker Spaniel is an art that requires a lot of practice to perfect, but you can learn the fundamentals and achieve good results.

enced groomers. Many attend grooming seminars, and a few are even certified by professional grooming associations.

Your Cocker is the best judge of any groomer. Is she clean, unharmed, and well-groomed when you pick her up? Does she seem confident around the groomer when she returns for her next visit?

Brushing

Whether you use a professional groomer or not, you need to do your part by brushing your dog at home. Regular brushing is the single most important factor in Cocker Spaniel coat care. Optimally you should do it every day. Realistically, try for two to three times a week. Schedule your grooming sessions for a regular time, perhaps during a favorite television show, so you both look forward to it as a time of quiet bonding. This will be possible only if your dog has learned that grooming is pleasant, and she won't learn this if you put it off until each session is a mat-pulling marathon. It's easiest if your dog is trained to lie on her side, either on a towel on the floor or sofa, or better, on a grooming table. You can do much of the brushing with her lying down, and then have her stand for the finishing touches.

Brushes

A pin brush is best for most brushing. A slicker brush, which is a brush with many fine bent wires, is also

ing noose, but it should not be so short that the dog is on its tiptoes. A dog left alone in these circumstances can meet with serious, even fatal, accidents. She can jump from the table and hang from the grooming noose, or can become fatally overheated in a closed cage with hot air blowing on her, especially if the groomer forgets the dog is in there.

Ask the groomer about experience, including where and how she learned to groom and how long she's been in business. Many excellent groomers are self-taught, but you don't want them to learn on your dog. Professional groomers often have graduated from dog-grooming schools or apprenticed under experi-

Brush down to the skin to remove all tangles.

good but not suggested if you're trying to save the coat. It's best to first mist the coat before brushing, which prevents coat breakage and cuts down on tangle-causing static electricity. You can use a spray conditioner or a weak mixture of conditioner and water.

How to Brush

Brush with the growth of the coat. Cockers have thick coats, so it's very important to brush below the surface. Start with the bottom areas of the coat, such as the bottom of the leg or chest. Lift the overlying coat out of the way and brush the remaining layer up to its root. Once that is tangle-free, move up to the next thin layer of coat, repeating until you reach the topmost layer.

Cottony coats can be difficult to deal with and can often benefit from a light application of a spray condi-

tioner or mink oil. It's best to spray the conditioner or oil on a brush you dedicate for this purpose, and then brush the dog with it. This will distribute the conditioner more thoroughly.

Tangles and Mats

Before moving to the next layer, you can use a coarse-toothed, then fine-toothed comb to ensure that no tangles are hiding. Soft, cottony coats are more prone to tangling than are silkier coats. Mats tend to form first under the elbows and beneath the ears, but they can form anywhere. Don't forget to check between the toes.

Use your fingers to ease out knots. Spraying tangles first with a detangler, or even packing them with cornstarch, may help. Larger tangles and mats may need to be picked apart with a steel comb or a mat-breaker. Pull the hair out of the mat rather than the mat out of the hair. Pull a large mat apart lengthwise and then work on each half. Continue to pull it apart until you have several tiny mats. Be sure to brush out each tiny mat until it is as smooth as the rest of the coat.

Cutting Out Mats

Resist the urge to reach for the scissors. The cut area will look ragged, and the shorter hair seems more prone to mat again. There are limits, however. It's no kindness to demat an extensively matted dog. Such a dog is better taken to an experienced groomer who will carefully clip the mats away. The matting may be so tight that it takes considerable skill to clip it out without nicking the skin. The skin beneath a mat that has been there a while may be unhealthy and so may break and bleed easily. The skin may be bruised from the constant pulling of the mats as they bunch tighter and tighter together with time. After the matting is removed, the area must be bathed with a soothing shampoo and treated with a good coat conditioner.

If you must cut out a mat on your own, snug a comb between the mat and the skin. This will place a barrier there so you won't accidentally cut your dog's skin, which is extremely easy to do otherwise.

You can't ignore mats. They won't go away on their own, and they only get worse. They bind the dog in a tattered straitjacket that inhibits her movement, invites skin disease, and repulses people.

Be sure to brush your dog thoroughly before bathing her. Bathing a tangled coat will only turn tangles into mats and set mats tighter.

Making Your Spaniel Spick-and-Span

Set aside an hour each week for bathing your Cocker. Dirt and oil form the foundation of mats, so if you want a mat-free coat, keeping it clean is an important step. Besides natural accumulation of oil from the skin (especially around the ear base), dirt and mud can gather in the feet and leg hair, food can get stuck to the ear tips, fecal matter can get caught in the britches, and urine can soak into the side coat—all creating a stew of fragrances that make your Cocker too smelly to cuddle.

You can use a rinse-free shampoo in a spritzer bottle to spot-clean problem areas if you need to postpone a full bath. Eventually, though, you won't be able put it off any longer. Gather together what you'll need before you corral your Cocker.

Shampoo

Humans and dogs require shampoos with different pH levels for optimal results because each is formulated to work best with different pH levels of hair. Human hair has a pH of 5.5, whereas dog hair has a pH of 7.0. Using a shampoo made for more acidic hair can eventually dry out the hair. Don't judge a shampoo by its suds. Sometimes more suds simply means more residue. There is no best shampoo for all Cockers, since they come in different coat types; also, the shampoo will interact with how hard your water is.

Cream Rinse

A good cream rinse will help your Cocker's hair lie more smoothly and be more manageable. A silkier coat requires less cream rinse than does a cottony coat. Although human cream rinses will work, those formulated for dogs work better. A conditioner is better than a cream rinse because it treats the hair shaft rather than simply coating it.

Tub

You'll need a hand sprayer so you can get water to all parts of your dog. The easiest way to bathe a dog is in a raised tub, but few people have that luxury. You should, however, make sure the surface your dog is standing on isn't slippery. Put a strainer over the drain so it doesn't get clogged with hair.

Prepping Your Cocker

If your dog's ears need to be cleaned, now is a good time to do it. Ear cleanser and debris can be messy, but you can wash away much of the mess if done before the bath. You can place cotton balls in the ear to try to keep water out, but realistically this usually just leads to ears with sopping-wet cotton balls in them. If the ears do get wet, place a drying agent, usually something containing

Teach your Cocker from an early age to enjoy bath time by giving him small mini-baths accompanied by lots of treats.

alcohol, in them so they don't remain wet. However, if your dog has ear problems and there is any chance of a ruptured eardrum, never put anything, especially anything containing alcohol, in the ear.

Many people suggest placing ophthalmic ointment in the eyes to keep out shampoo, but the trend now is to avoid this step. Rather than protect the eye, the ointment may trap some irritants and prevent the dog's tears

A "snood" is handy for keeping the ears from dragging in the food when your Cocker eats.

from cleansing the eyes. Instead, just be careful when bathing and rinsing around the eyes, or better, use a tearless shampoo in that area.

The Bath

Begin the bath by wetting your dog down to the skin with warm water. Holding her ears will often cut down on how often she shakes water all over you, as will holding the nozzle close to her skin, even touching it. Mix about one part shampoo to ten parts water and then apply it to the coat. Gently distribute the shampoo all over her body, making sure it reaches down to the skin.

Rinse and repeat. You can use a sponge to rinse the face. Be especially thorough in your second rins-

ing. Shampoo left in the coat can cause dry skin and itching. When rinsing the face, gently hold the head upward toward the ceiling, but not too high, to prevent water from going up the nose.

Next apply the cream rinse or conditioner, leaving it on for a few minutes. Again, rinse thoroughly, although a little conditioner left in may be helpful if your dog's coat is dry.

Drying

Once you're through rinsing, step back and allow your dog to shake. She may refuse, waiting until you've let her out of the tub so she can douse your bathroom in the process, so you may wish to cover her with a towel and hustle her to a better place. Give her a chance to shake, then use your hands to squeeze the excess water from her coat. Next, towel dry her, taking care not to rub so vigorously that you create tangles. You'll probably need several towels.

Once you let her loose she's going to celebrate by dashing about crazily. If she's outside, she'll run around and collect dirt on her wet feet and underside, which will turn to mud. If she's inside, she'll run around and slip on any tile floors you have. Because you've wet her down to the skin, she's likely to be become chilled more than she would had she simply gotten wet in the rain or from swimming, so keep her in a warm area.

Blow-drying

The next step is blow-drying. If possible, invest in a forced-air dryer. Your own blow-dryer relies on blowing heated air to dry your hair. A forced-air dryer blows unheated air at high velocity. It dries faster, and with less chance of burning your dog's skin. The cost is about $100. You can use a hot-air blow-dryer; just be careful that you don't overheat the skin or hair. Make yourself comfortable; this is going to take a while. Start by having your dog stand in front of the dryer, moving the dryer so you gradually get the coat damp rather than wet. At this point she can lie down and you can really get to work. Begin drying from the bottom, lifting the hair in layers just as you do when brushing her. While doing this, brush the hair in the direction it grows, which will help remove any

curling. If the hair dries and curls before you can get to it, you can mist it and do it over.

Once your dog is completely dry, brush through her coat one last time to make sure no tangles have appeared. Then take her picture, because as soon as she can she's going to shake and then roll around in the dirt.

Do-It-Yourself Trimming Guide

You may prefer to learn to groom your Cocker yourself. If you want to groom your Cocker for show, you'll find that most dog groomers don't offer, and in fact aren't trained to do, show trimming. That means you'll need to have an experienced spaniel person teach you, and probably prepare your dog for you at first. That's one reason buying from a local breeder is important if you plan to show your dog.

Even for a pet trim it's best to have a couple of hands-on lessons from a person experienced with spaniels. Assuming that's not possible, you can teach yourself. Just expect to make some mistakes at first.

Your major outlays will be a good grooming table and good clippers. A grooming table is handy to have anyway for brushing, but it's essential for trimming. It should have a grooming arm to which you can attach a noose to hold your dog in place. Never leave her unattended with her head in the noose, because she could jump off, possibly hanging herself.

Clippers

Buy good clippers. Those that sell for $20 tend to cut so poorly that you will only be frustrated. Good clippers have easily interchangeable blades and sell for about $100. You'll have to buy several blades as well. Blades are numbered according to how closely they cut, with higher numbers indicating a closer cut. Most clippers come with a #10 blade, and that's a handy, fairly close-cutting blade that you will use a lot with a Cocker. You may also want a #15 blade for doing the face, ears, throat, and paw pads, although a #10 blade will also work for these areas. A #7F blade (F means finishing; these are good for blending areas of shorter and longer hair) is handy for doing the back, sides, and neck. Some groomers prefer a #8½ blade for the neck, and a #5F or #4F blade for the back and sides.

Trim in the direction of the arrows.

In general, the sparser and softer the coat, the longer the cutting blade (lower number) you want to use. This is doubly true if your dog has sensitive skin. If you use a blade that cuts too short, especially if you work against the direction of hair growth, you increase the odds of creating a painful situation called razor burn. When you use a blade that cuts close, you must be extremely vigilant not to cut the skin. Holding the skin taut to remove any folds will lessen the chances.

You will also need to buy some good-quality scissors and thinning shears. If you were grooming for show, you would additionally want several stripping tools. Stripping tools leave the hair looking natural, not clipped, and usually leave it slightly harder than clipped hair. You should ask your breeder how to use a stripping tool if you decide you want to go for a show look.

How Much to Trim?

If you want a utilitarian coat that will need the least upkeep, you can shave your Cocker all over. You can use a #10 blade, but you'll probably get better results with a #8½ blade. If, however, you prefer a Cocker trim, you can use the following guidelines. Note that as a general rule, you should clip in the direction of hair growth.

Muzzle

Clip the entire muzzle, including the chin, cheeks, and top of nose, using a #10 blade. Extend the clipped area in an upside-down V-pattern with the apex between the eyebrows, and running below each eye so that it extends behind the eye on the lower cheek area. Hold the skin fairly tight if necessary to prevent folds where it could be cut.

Topskull

You can also use the #10 blade to clip the area on the backskull between the ears and to the occiput. One of the most difficult areas to master is above the brows, which should be long enough so that it emphasizes the deep stop. Use thinning shears to round it, taking off enough hair so that it doesn't flop over but leaving enough on so that it gives the dog a rounded forehead. Use the thinning shears to blend it into the shorter hair of the backskull.

Ears

Clip the top third of the entire length (not just the leather) of the ear using a #10 blade. Start from the top of the ear and work down to end not in a horizontal line, but in a V-shape. You may find it easier to do this if you hold the ear flat in your hand.

Use a #10 blade to clip the inside of the ear. Follow the same pattern you set on the outside of the ear.

Use scissors to carefully trim the remaining hairs hanging below the ear leather. Don't cut them straight across, but round them slightly.

Note: Once you are experienced, you can use a #15 blade for a shorter cut on the muzzle and ears,

Trimming the head requires more precision.

but it carries a greater risk of creating razor burn. Start with a #10 blade.

Neck

Use a #10 blade from the lips down to the breastbone (be careful not to cut the lips, especially the part that is somewhat loose and fleshy). You may wish to pull the ears forward to get them out of your way. You can clip against the grain of the hair to get a close cut here. End in a V-shape at the breastbone.

Use a lower-number blade, such as a #8½ or #7F, for the sides and top of the neck, where the hair should be slightly longer. Again, be very careful around any loose folds. Clip the lower sides of the neck to the level of the breastbone, working so that the line follows the contours of the shoulder blade.

Back

The hair on the back should be close. For show grooming, this means using stripping knives and thinning tools. For everyday pet grooming, it's much easier to use a clipper, probably a #5F, #7F, or #8½ blade. Some groomers find good results using a #7F blade against the grain for the back. Clip in the direction of hair growth, trying to make as smooth a line as possible from shoulders to tail tip. Clip down the sides to the point at which the long hair starts to hang straight down, or around a visual line drawn between the breastbone and pelvic bone. Overlapping your strokes will help hide ridges from the clipper marks. Try to stop at the same point without leaving a definite line. With experience you will be able to gradually lift the clippers away from the coat so you don't leave a definite line. Use thinning shears to blend any clipped areas into areas of longer furnishings.

Note that many older Cockers grow warts that may occur on the back. Using a blade that cuts too short can also cut the warts, which you don't want to happen. A #8½ blade will usually be safe for these dogs.

Underside

When grooming for show, the coat is usually left fairly long, and great care is taken to blend the coat from the bottom of the legs into the chest and loin so it all flows as a rounded line. When grooming for everyday, you'll probably want to trim the underside much shorter. Use scissors to trim the coat to a manageable length, keeping it slightly longer under the chest.

For pet clips, trim the hair under the elbows, along the stomach, and inside the thighs. Done carefully, this should not show when the dog is viewed from the side, as the longer side furnishings should cover it. It will help prevent matting, however, and make the coat easier to maintain.

Clean the hair from the area around the anus, either with a #10 blade or thinning shears.

Legs

Normally you would leave the legs untrimmed. However, you can still have a Cocker look by trimming the legs with a #4 or #5 blade.

Feet

You have a choice of several ways of trimming the feet. One method is to lift the hair of the lower leg up out of the way and use the #10 blade to trim the toes or even the entire foot. Then let the leg hair down so it drapes over it. Next, trim the bottom of the leg hair so it's off the ground. This cut prevents the coat from getting too messy with dirt and leaves.

A more difficult trim is the one favored for show Cockers. It has a beveled appearance, so that the rear of the leg above the foot sweeps upward in a slight curve. Start with both front and rear feet by cutting the hair between the pads, using either scissors or a #10 blade.

For the front foot bevel, hold the foot up and comb the hair over the foot, then use scissors to cut the hair at the level of or just above the pads. Hold the scissors at a slight angle so

Hot Spots

A hot spot, technically known as pyrotraumatic dermatitis, is an area of skin that is irritated, perhaps by a flea bite, so that the dog scratches or chews it. It quickly becomes enlarged, infected, and painful. Treat by clipping away hair and cleansing the area with surgical soap. Some people find that washing with Listerine gives good results. Apply an antibiotic cream or, better, an antibiotic powder. Prevent the dog from further chewing and scratching.

that the hair is cut slightly shorter toward the outside. Curved scissors work best for this. Next, place the foot in a standing position and scissor around the outside, continuing the line you just started. Hold the scissors at an angle so the hair is shorter near the foot and longer further up on the leg.

For the rear foot bevel, begin as you did with the front foot, cutting the hair from between the pads and around the foot. Hold the foot up behind your dog to do this. Angle the area behind the foot upward toward the point of the hock so the hair gets gradually longer as it goes higher on the leg. The bevels take a lot of practice, but if you mess up, you can always cut them shorter!

Trim First

Trim your Cocker before bathing her. Otherwise you end up bathing and drying a lot of hair you're going to cut off anyway. The bathing will also help the trimmed hair appear smoother and more natural. After bathing and drying you can come back and do some fine tuning.

External Parasites

In times past, small dogs, especially toy spaniels, were used to attract fleas from their owners. Nowadays the tables are turned, and it's your job to debug your dog.

Fleas

Fleas are an age-old curse that only recently have been on the losing side. In the past, dog owners sprayed their dogs and yards with poisons until it seemed the people and dogs might die before the fleas did. It was expensive, time-consuming, and potentially dangerous Newer products have a higher initial purchase price but are cheaper in the long run because they work and need be reapplied only every few months. Most of these products are available only from your veterinarian, although some discount products try to sound as if they work the same way. Look for a product with one of the following ingredients:

• *imidacloprid*, a self-distributing liquid that kills fleas within a day and continues for a month. It can withstand water, but not repeated bathing.

• *fipronil*, a spray or self-distributing liquid that collects in the hair follicles and wicks out over time. It kills fleas for up to three months and ticks for

Consider a practical short trim for dogs that spend a lot of time outside.

a shorter time, and is resistant to bathing.

• *selamectin*, a self-distributing liquid that kills fleas for one month. It also kills ear mites and several internal parasites, and acts as a heartworm preventive.

• *nytenpyram*, oral medication that starts killing fleas in twenty minutes; all fleas are killed in four hours. It has almost no residual activity, so it's mostly for a quick fix of heavily infested dogs.

• *lufenuron, methoprene*, and *fenoxycarb*, chemicals that render any fleas that bite the dog sterile.

Most over-the-counter products are permethrin-based, which isn't resistant to water and doesn't kill fleas for long. Flea populations can easily become resistant to it. In fact, fleas can become resistant to any treatment, so the best strategy is to change products frequently and to include the use of both a flea killer and a flea sterilizer.

Ticks

Ticks are harder to kill. The same fipronil flea product will kill ticks, but not immediately. Amitraz tick collars are also effective, but not perfect. No matter what, if you're in a tick-infested area you'll need to feel your Cocker for these pest daily (she'll like the extra petting), paying close attention around her ears, neck, and between her toes. To remove a tick, use a tissue or tweezers and grasp the tick as close to the skin as possible. Pull slowly, trying not to lose the head or squeeze the contents back into the dog. Even if you get the head with the tick, it will often leave a bump for several days.

Ticks can transmit several diseases. A vaccination is available for Lyme disease, but it's not advisable for dogs that don't live in Lyme-endemic areas, and in fact may not even be advisable for those that do live in such areas. This is a question for your veterinarian. Of greater concern is erhlichiosis, a potentially fatal disease that cripples the immune

Healthy dogs should smell good. Grooming entails not only coat and skin care, but also nail, tooth, eye, and ear care.

system and often has vague symptoms. Other tick-borne diseases include Rocky Mountain Spotted Fever and babesiosis. Your veterinarian can order blood tests if these conditions are suspected.

Mites

Mites can also cause problems. Sarcoptic mites cause sarcoptic mange, an intensely itchy disorder that humans can catch. It's often characterized by small bumps and crusts on the ear tips, abdomen, elbows, and hocks. The condition can be treated with repeated shampoos or with an injection.

Demodex mites cause demodectic mange, a noncontagious but one that is often difficult to treat. A couple of small patches in a puppy are commonplace and will usually go away on their own, but many such patches or a generalized condition must be treated with repeated dips or with drug therapy. Cases involving the feet can be especially difficult to cure.

Another type of mite, the ear mite, is discussed under ear care (page 102).

The Pedicure

An important part of your Cocker's beauty treatment is actually also an important health precaution. Nails that grow too long can get caught in carpet loops and pulled from the nail

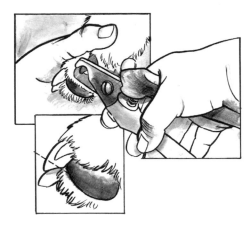

Cut the tip of the nail, avoiding the sensitive quick. You can see the pink quick in a light colored nail. In a dark nail, look beneath it and cut only the part that is hollow.

bed. They impact the ground with every step, displacing the normal position of the toes and causing discomfort, splaying, and even lameness. If dewclaws, those rudimentary "thumbs" on the wrists, are present, they are especially prone to getting caught on things and ripped out, and can even grow in a loop and back into the leg. These are especially easy to forget about when covered by the Cocker's long leg coat.

Unfortunately, some dogs seem to think you're cutting off not only their nails, but also their toes. You have to convince them from the time they are puppies that this is worth the treats you will be heaping on them for every nail cut. Do this enough, and avoid cutting the quick, and your Cocker will be wishing she had more toes. Use nail clippers—the guillotine type are usually easier—and be sure they are sharp. Dull clippers crush the nail and hurt. You can also use a tiny nail grinder, but don't let the heat build up, and don't let the long hair

wrap around the shaft. The way to avoid this is by putting an old nylon stocking over the foot and pushing each nail through it before filing.

There are several ways to see where the quick, the sensitive and potentially bleeding part of the nail, stops. If you look under the nail you can see where it begins to get hollow; anywhere it looks hollow is quickless. In this same area the nail will suddenly get much thinner. Again, where it's thin it's safe to cut. In a light-colored nail you can see a redder area that indicates the blood supply; the sensitive quick extends slightly farther down the nail than the blood supply. When in doubt, cut too little and gradually whittle your way higher. You'll eventually goof up and cut the quick. That calls for styptic powder to quell the bleeding and lots of extra treats to assuage your guilt!

Dental Care

Cockers shed their baby (deciduous) teeth between 4 and 7 months of age. Sometimes some of them, especially the canine teeth, don't fall out and the permanent teeth grow in alongside them. That's not uncommon for a few days, but if it persists for a week or more, ask your veterinarian if the baby tooth may have to be extracted. Otherwise it can dis-

Well-groomed Cockers are among the world's most stunning dogs.

place the permanent teeth and affect the occlusion.

Dental care begins in puppyhood as you teach your Cocker to enjoy getting her teeth brushed. You can use a soft bristle toothbrush and meat-flavored doggy toothpaste. Because dogs don't spit, the foaming agents in human toothpaste can make them feel sick, and the high sodium content of baking powder is unhealthy. Besides, how many people toothpastes are meat flavored? Brush a little, and give a treat. Ideally, teeth should be brushed once a day. Realistically, once a week is better than never.

If you let plaque build up, it attracts bacteria and minerals, which harden into tartar. The tartar spreads rootward, causing irreversible periodontal disease with tissue, bone, and tooth loss. The bacteria gain an inlet to the bloodstream, where they can cause kidney and heart valve infections.

Hard, crunchy foods can help, but they won't take the place of brushing. If tartar accumulates, your Cocker may need a through cleaning under anesthesia. You wouldn't think of going days, weeks, months, or even years without brushing your teeth. Why would you expect your dog to?

Chapter Eight
Cocker Clinic

Your Cocker is only human. Like you, she'll get sick occasionally. Unlike you, she won't be able to tell anybody where it hurts. By knowing the signs of illness, when to call the veterinarian, and how to be a doggy nurse, you can walk that line between being a negligent and hypochondriac dog owner.

Signs of Sickness

Choose a veterinarian before your dog is sick. Consider availability, emergency arrangements, facilities, costs, ability to communicate, and experience with Cockers—which most veterinarians have in abundance. Most general veterinarians can provide a wide range of services, but if your Cocker has a problem that eludes diagnosis or requires specialized treatment, let your veterinarian know if you are willing to be referred to a specialist in that field.

Being the link between your dog and his doctor is not easy. Since your dog can't talk, you have to interpret his behavioral and physical signs.

Behavior Changes

Sick dogs often lie quietly in a curled position. Dogs with pain may be irritable or restless, and may hide, claw, pant, or tremble. Dogs with abdominal pain often stretch and bow. A dog with breathing difficulties may refuse to lie down, or if he does, will keep his head raised.

Cockers are champions of the ring, field, and heart.

Lethargy is the most common sign of illness. Possible causes include
- Infection (check for fever)
- Anemia (check gum color)
- Circulatory problem (check pulse and gum color)
- Pain (check limbs, neck, back, mouth, eyes, ears, and abdomen for signs)
- Nausea
- Poisoning (check gum color and pupil reaction; look for vomiting or abdominal pain)
- Sudden vision loss
- Cancer
- Metabolic diseases

Intake and Output Changes

Changes in eating, drinking, or elimination patterns often indicate illness. Loss of appetite is most often associated with illness, although increased appetite may accompany some endocrine disorders. Increased thirst, usually with increased urination, may indicate kidney disease or diabetes.

Urinating small amounts frequently, often with some sign of pain, may indicate a urinary tract infection. Painful urination, straining to urinate, or blood in the urine may indicate urinary stones. Inability to urinate is a life-threatening emergency.

Vomiting food after it's been in the stomach can indicate poisoning, blockage, or a host of problems. Consult your veterinarian immediately if your dog vomits feces-like matter (which could indicate an intestinal blockage) or blood (which may resemble coffee grounds), has accompanying fever or pain, or if the vomiting lasts more than a few hours. Regurgitating food right after eating can indicate an esophageal problem.

Diarrhea can result from nervousness, a change in diet or water, food sensitivities, intestinal parasites, infections, poisoning, or many illnesses. It's not uncommon for dogs to have blood in their diarrhea, but diarrhea with lots of blood, or accompanied by vomiting, fever, or other symptoms of illness, warrants a call to the veterinarian. Bright red blood indicates a source lower in the digestive tract, while dark black tarry stools indicate a source higher in the digestive tract, and is often of greater concern.

Coughing

Coughing can be caused by foreign bodies, kennel cough, and heart disease, among others. Congestive heart failure causes coughing and breathing difficulties mainly after exercise and at night and early morning. Kennel cough is a communicable airborne disease caused by several infectious agents. It is characterized by a gagging or honking cough, often a week after being around infected dogs. Any cough lasting longer than a few days or accompanied by weakness or difficulty breathing warrants a veterinary exam.

Physical Changes

Sometimes you need to check over your dog piece by piece.

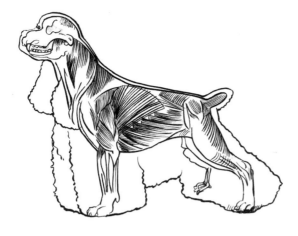

oxygen. Bright red gums may indicate overheating or carbon monoxide poisoning, and yellow gums can indicate jaundice. Tiny red splotches may indicate a blood-clotting problem. Tooth and gum problems will often cause bad breath and pain.

Eyes. Squinting or pawing at the eye can arise from pain. Swelling and redness may indicate glaucoma, a scratched cornea, or several other problems. Profuse tear discharge may be caused by a foreign body, scratched cornea, or blocked tear drainage duct. Thick mucus and a dull-appearing surface may indicate "dry eye" (keratoconjunctivitis sicca, or KCS). See page 95 for descriptions of hereditary eye problems.

Ears. Inflamed, painful, or itchy ears can result from infection or parasites. See page 71 for more about ear health.

Feet. Foot problems can account for limping. Cut long or split nails short (see page 80), and protect cut pads. Swollen toes could be from infection or an orthopedic problem.

Mouth. If you think your Cocker is sick, one of the first things to check is his gum color. Gums should be a deep pink, and if you press with your thumb, they should return to pink within two seconds after lifting your thumb (a longer time suggests a circulatory problem). Very pale gums may indicate anemia, shock, or poor circulation. Bluish gums or tongue can mean a life-threatening lack of

Skin. Parasites, allergies, and infections can cause many skin problems (see page 100). Lumps in the skin may or may not be serious but warrant a veterinary examination.

Anus. Repeated diarrhea can cause an irritated anal area. Repeated scooting or licking can be from diarrhea, parasites, or especially, impacted anal sacs. These are

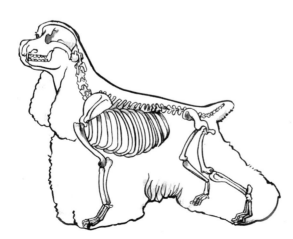

The Five Minute Checkup

Make several copies of this checklist and keep a record of your dog's home exams.

Date: _____

Weight: _____

Temperature: _____

Pulse: _____

Behavior

Is your dog
- ☐ Restless? ☐ Lethargic?
- ☐ Weak? ☐ Dizzy?
- ☐ Irritable? ☐ Confused?
- ☐ Bumping into things?
- ☐ Trembling?
- ☐ Pacing?
- ☐ Hiding? ____
- ☐ Eating more or less than usual?
- ☐ Drinking more than usual?
- ☐ Urinating more or less than usual, or with straining?
- ☐ Having diarrhea?
- ☐ Straining to defecate?
- ☐ Just standing with front feet on ground and rear in the air?
- ☐ Vomiting or trying to vomit?
- ☐ Regurgitating undigested food?
- ☐ Gagging?
- ☐ Coughing?
- ☐ Breathing rapidly at rest?
- ☐ Spitting up froth?
- ☐ Pawing at throat?
- ☐ Snorting?
- ☐ Limping?

Physical Exam

Hydration: ☐ Dry, sticky gums?
- ☐ Skin that doesn't pop back when stretched?

Gum color: ☐ Pink (good) ☐ Bright red
- ☐ Bluish ☐ Whitish ☐ Red spots

Gums: ☐ Swellings? ☐ Bleeding?
- ☐ Sores? ☐ Growths?

Teeth: ☐ Loose? ☐ Painful? ☐ Dirty?
- ☐ Bad breath?

Nose: ☐ Thick or colored discharge?
- ☐ Cracking? ☐ Pinched? ☐ Sores?

Eyes: ☐ Tearing? ☐ Mucous discharge?
- ☐ Dull surface? ☐ Squinting?
- ☐ Swelling? ☐ Redness?
- ☐ Unequal pupils? ☐ Pawing at eyes?

Ears: ☐ Bad smell? ☐ Redness?
- ☐ Abundant debris? ☐ Scabby ear tips?
- ☐ Head shaking? ☐ Head tilt?
- ☐ Ear scratching? ☐ Painfulness?

Feet: ☐ Long or split nails? ☐ Cut pads?
- ☐ Swollen or misaligned toes?

Skin: ☐ Parasites?
- ☐ Black grains (flea dirt)? ☐ Hair loss?
- ☐ Scabs? ☐ Greasy patches?
- ☐ Bad odor? ☐ Lumps?

Anal and genital regions:
- ☐ Swelling? ☐ Discharge?
- ☐ Redness? ☐ Bloody urine?
- ☐ Bloody or blackened diarrhea?
- ☐ Worms in stool or around anus?
- ☐ Scooting rear? ☐ Licking rear?

Abdomen: ☐ Bloating?

Body: ☐ Asymmetrical bones or muscles?
- ☐ Lumps? ☐ Weight change?

If you answered "yes" to anything abnormal in the checklist, it's worth a call to your veterinarian. Refer to the text for more information.

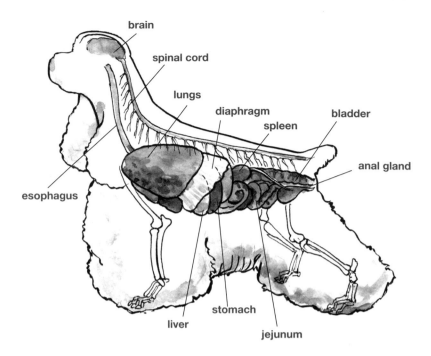

brain

spinal cord

lungs

diaphragm

spleen

bladder

anal gland

esophagus

stomach

liver

jejunum

The internal organs.

two sacs filled with smelly brown liquid that normally is excreted with the feces or in times of fright. In some cases the material can't get out. The sac becomes uncomfortably distended, sometimes becoming infected. It may swell outward, even appearing to be a tumor, and often finally bursting. Your veterinarian can manually express the contents.

Pulse

To check the pulse, cup your hand around the top of your dog's rear leg so your fingers are near the top, almost where the leg joins the body. Feel for the pulse in the femoral artery. Normal adult Cocker pulse rate is 70 to 120 beats per minute.

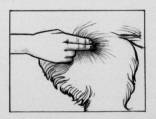

Feel the pulse in the femoral artery inside the thigh, just below where it joins the trunk.

Hydration

Check hydration by touching the gums, which should be slick, not sticky, or by lifting the skin on the back and letting it go. It should snap back into place quickly, not remain tented. Sticky gums and tented skin indicate dehydration. If your dog has been vomiting or has diarrhea, she may instantly lose any water you give her, in which case your veterinarian may need to give your dog fluids.

Blood Tests

Your veterinarian will often order various blood tests if your dog is ill. These tests are a vital part of the diagnosis.

A Complete Blood Count (CBC) is the basic test your veterinarian will call for, especially if your dog just feels under the weather. It includes values for red blood cells and some form of white blood cells. Abnormal values of red blood cells can indicate various types of anemia, or in some cases, dehydration. Abnormal values of white blood cells can indicate infections and give an idea about whether or not the infection is chronic. A platelet count may also be included; from it, your veterinarian can see if your dog has a platelet deficiency that may cause a clotting disorder, or if internal bleeding, for example, has recently used up a lot of platelets.

Various blood chemistry tests also provide a wealth of information. Ele-

Temperature

To take your dog's temperature, lubricate a rectal thermometer and insert it about 2 inches (5 cm) into the dog's anus, leaving it there for about a minute. Normal is from 101°F to 102°F. If the temperature is

• 103°F or above, call your veterinarian for advice. This is not usually an emergency.

• 105°F or above, go to your veterinarian. This is probably an emergency; 106°F or above is dangerous. Try to cool your dog by sponging with cool water in front of a fan.

• 98°F or below, called your veterinarian for advice. Try to warm your dog with towels warmed in the microwave.

• 96°F or below, go to your veterinarian. Treat for hypothermia on the way by warming your dog.

vated blood urea nitrogen (BUN), creatinine (CREA), and phosphorus (PHOS) suggest kidney disease. Elevated calcium (CA) can also suggest kidney disease, as well as parathyroid or some tumors. Elevated cholesterol (CHOL) or reduced albumin (ALB) can indicate kidney or liver disease. Low blood glucose (GLU) can indicate liver disease. Elevated alanine aminotransferase (ALT) or alkaline phosphatase (ALKP) suggests liver disease. Specialized tests exist for a multitude of other disorders.

Lethargy is cause for investigation.

Urine tests are important, too, in diagnosing many diseases, especially diabetes and kidney disease.

Medications

Never give your Cocker human medications unless your veterinarian tells you to. Some human medications work on dogs but must be used at different strengths, and others have no effect or bad effects on dogs. Always give the full course of any medication your veterinarian prescribes, even if your dog appears well; otherwise, the problem can return and may be more resistant next time.

To give a pill, open your dog's mouth and place the pill well in the rear. Close the mouth and gently stroke the throat until she swallows. Or just hide the pill in some liverwurst or other soft treat and watch to make sure she eats it. To give liquid medication, place the liquid in the side of the mouth and let the dog swallow. Don't squirt it in so that the dog inhales it.

Emergencies

First aid doesn't take the place of veterinary attention. In every case described below, first call the veterinarian and then apply first aid as you're transporting the dog. Move the dog as little as possible, but get her in a safe place. Be ready to treat for shock.

Shock

Signs of shock are weakness, collapse, pale gums, unresponsiveness, and faint pulse. Because shock may occur in almost any case of trauma, it's usually best to treat the dog as though she were experiencing this conidtion. Keep her warm and quiet, and keep her head low in relation to the position of her heart (unless she has a head wound).

Heatstroke

Early signs of heatstroke include rapid loud breathing, abundant thick saliva, bright red mucous membranes, and high rectal temperature. Later signs include unsteadiness, diarrhca, and coma.

Wet the dog down and place her in front of a fan. If this isn't possible, immerse her in cold water, but don't plunge her in ice water, because that constricts the peripheral blood vessels so much that they can't cool the blood efficiently. Instead, offer her water to drink.

You must lower your dog's body temperature quickly, but don't let it go below 100°F. Stop cooling when the rectal temperature reaches 103°F, because it will continue to fall.

Even when her temperature is back to normal, your Cocker is still in danger and still needs veterinary attention. It will take several days for

The First-Aid Kit

- Emergency veterinary phone number
- First-aid instructions
- Rectal thermometer
- Scissors
- Sterile gauze dressings
- Self-adhesive bandage
- Antiseptic skin ointment
- Instant cold compress
- Antidiarrheal medication
- Allergy medication
- Ophthalmic ointment
- Penlight
- Hydrogen peroxide
- Activated charcoal
- Tongue depressor
- Soap

your dog to recover, during which time she should not exert herself.

Bleeding

To control bleeding, cover the wound with clean dressing and apply pressure. Add more dressings over any blood-soaked bandages until the bleeding stops. Elevating the wound site and applying a cold pack to the

Pressure points to slow bleeding from extremities.

area will also slow bleeding. If the wound is on a front leg, apply pressure to the inside just above the elbow. If it's on a rear leg, apply pressure inside the thigh where the femoral artery crosses the thigh bone.

Stings

Insect stings can sometimes cause allergic reactions such as swelling around the nose and throat, which can block the airways. Other possible reactions include restlessness, vomiting, diarrhea, seizures, and collapse. At the slightest hint of a reaction, give your dog an allergy pill (ask your veterinarian for the best type to keep in your first-aid kit and how much to administer).

Seizures

A dog having a seizure may drool, stiffen, yelp, or twitch uncontrollably. Wrap the dog in a blanket and keep her away from stairs and other dogs.

Never put your hands or anything else in a convulsing dog's mouth. Make note of everything you can remember about the seizure and what the dog did; doing so may help determine the cause.

Poisoning

Signs of poisoning vary according to the type of poison, but often include vomiting, depression, and convulsions. When in doubt, call your veterinarian or an animal poison control hotline (see page 148). If the poison was ingested in the past two hours, and if it's not an acid, alkali, petroleum product, solvent, or tranquilizer, you may be advised to induce vomiting by giving hydrogen peroxide or dry mustard mixed 1:1 with water. Ipecac syrup is not recommended for this purpose in dogs. In other cases you may be advised to dilute the poison by giving milk or vegetable oil. Activated charcoal can adsorb many toxins. Poisons act in different ways, so it's important to have the label of any suspected poisons available. Here is a list of a few that could harm your dog:
• Ethylene glycol–based antifreeze is a dog killer. Even tiny amounts cause irreversible kidney damage, and the prognosis is poor once symptoms appear. Get emergency help if you suspect your dog has consumed antifreeze.

- Rodent poisons are either warfarin-based, causing uncontrolled internal bleeding, or cholecalciferol-based, which cause kidney failure.
- Bird and squirrel poisons are usually strychnine-based and cause neurological malfunction.
- Insect poisons, weed killers, and wood preservatives may be arsenic-based and cause kidney failure.
- Flea, tick, and internal parasite poisons may contain organophosphates, which can cause neurological symptoms.
- Iron-based rose fertilizers can cause kidney and liver failure.

The Older Cocker

Old age is the reward of good genes, good care, and good luck. Cocker Spaniels have an average life span of 12 to 15 years. Older Cockers still needs lots of mental and physical stimulation, but maybe not at the level they did as youngsters. Riding in the car, running laps in the house, and sniffing out birds in the backyard can fill an older dog's day.

In Tribute

One of the noblest tributes to a cherished Cocker Spaniel is to make a donation to a canine welfare organization such as a Cocker rescue group or health research facility, such as the Canine Health Foundation or the American Spaniel Club Foundation (see page 148).

Older dogs often have a hard time seeing and hearing. Cockers with vision loss can cope well as long as you keep them in familiar surroundings, place sound or scent beacons at key locations, and block off pools and steps. Those with hearing loss can learn to respond to hand signals, vibrating collars, and flashing lights if you use the same training techniques you did to teach voice commands.

Many older dogs suffer from cognitive dysfunction, in which they appear confused, depressed, or disoriented. Challenging their minds with games or new tricks every day can help stave it off. Your veterinarian can also prescribe drug therapy that may give good results.

Excessive weight places an added burden on the heart, back, and joints, but keeping an older Cocker svelte can be a challenge. Most healthy older dogs don't need a special diet, but they should receive high-quality protein. Moistening dry food or adding canned food can help dogs with dental problems enjoy their meals.

Bad breath, lip licking, reluctance to chew, or swelling around the mouth can all signal periodontal disease that should be addressed before it progresses further. A thorough tooth cleaning and perhaps drug therapy is needed.

Don't ignore stronger body odors, which can signal periodontal disease, impacted anal sacs, seborrhea, or ear infections. Regular brushing can help soothe dry, itchy skin by stimulating oil production. The nails tend to

A long life depends on good genes, good care, and good luck.

get especially long in older dogs, so you'll need to cut them more often.

Health

A senior Cocker should have a checkup twice a year. That's not excessive when you consider the rate at which your dog is aging. Tests can detect early stages of treatable diseases.

Arthritis slows many older dogs. Keeping weight down, providing a warm, soft bed, attending to injuries, and maintaining a program of low-impact exercise can help mild cases. Drugs and supplements can also help. Polysulfated glycosaminogly-can increases the compressive resilience of cartilage; glucosamine stimulates collagen synthesis and may help rejuvenate cartilage; and chondroitin sulfate helps shield cartilage from destructive enzymes. Anti-inflammatory drugs may help alleviate some pain, but must be used with veterinary supervision.

Older dogs may have less efficient immune systems, making it more important to shield them from infectious diseases or stress. However, if your Cocker stays home all the time she may not need to be vaccinated as often as when she was younger, but this is an area of controversy that you should discuss with your veterinarian.

Old dogs suffer from many of the same diseases that old people do. Cancer accounts for almost half the deaths of dogs over the age of 10 years; its signs include weight or appetite loss, collapse, swellings, lameness, difficulty swallowing, or lethargy, among others. Heart disease, often signaled by weakness, coughing, or fluid accumulation in the tissues of the limbs or belly, is also a major problem in older dogs. Kidney disease, signaled by increased thirst and urination, is yet another serious condition. Cushing's syndrome (hyper-adrenocorticism), too, is seen often in older dogs; its signs include increased hunger, thirst, and urination, as well as hair loss, muscle atrophy, and a potbelly. Your veterinarian can diagnose and treat most of these problems.

Chapter Nine
Hereditary Health

Every dog of every breed carries, on average, between five and seven deleterious recessives genes. The trick is making sure dogs carrying the same bad genes don't produce puppies that inherit them from both parents and thus may be affected by that disorder. The smaller the breed's gene pool and the more widespread that particular gene, the more difficult it is to avoid.

At first glance, Cockers appear to have more than their share of hereditary disorders. Part of the reason lies simply in numbers. With so many Cockers in the world, veterinarians have a chance to see trends in diseases and realize when they seem to run in families.

Another part of the problem lies with the careless breeding that accompanies popularity. If you contemplate breeding, don't repeat the mistakes of those naïve and unscrupulous breeders who have bred without knowledge of or concern for hereditary problems. Perform health testing on your dogs, understand the genetics behind any problems, and make sure you are not perpetuating a disorder that could cause heartache down the road.

Eye Diseases

Those soulful eyes are unfortunately prone to several hereditary problems. Your best prevention is to select your Cocker from dogs certified free of eye diseases for at least two generations, preferably with their siblings certified as well. Your second-best prevention is to be on the lookout for signs of eye problems before they get out of hand. The following list of Cocker-predisposed eye conditions starts at the front of the eye and works toward the rear.

Distichiasis. Eyelash hairs are supposed to grow just outside the margin of the eye rims, but sometimes they grow from abnormal locations in the lids and project toward the surface of the eye. When they touch the surface of the cornea they irritate the eye, especially if the lashes or hairs are coarse. Most Cockers have at least a few of these errant hairs, but fortunately they tend to be fine and don't always cause problems. If your Cocker has painful eyes, corneal ulcerations, or mucus discharge, it could be the result of distichiasis, but it is more likely caused by one of the other conditions to which Cockers are prone.

Ectropion and entropion. These two conditions refer to problems in eyelid configuration. *Ectropion* refers to lids that are turned out, usually a lower lid that puckers or droops. Cockers often have some degree of ectropion, but seldom severe cases. Because the puckered lid allows debris and dust to settle in the area between the lid and the eye, conjunctivitis often arises from it. Serious cases warrant surgical correction, in which a wedge of tissue is removed from the lid margin and the lid is stretched tight.

Entropion refers to lids that are turned in. In the Cocker, the type of entropion is lateral canthal, which means it usually affects the outer corner of both upper and lower lids. The inverted lids rub on the eye's surface and irritate it, causing redness, tearing, and sometimes, corneal ulceration. Surgery is the only treatment. A young puppy with entropion may have the lids tacked temporarily; sometimes they will then grow out of it. The mode of inheritance for both ectropion and entropion is unknown.

Cherry eye. Dogs have a third eyelid, or nictitating membrane, in the inner corner of each eye. Barely noticeable, it normally appears as a flat membrane stretched across the inner corner of the eyeball. In some dogs, mostly young ones, the tear gland at the base of the membrane becomes enlarged, pushing past the third eyelid and protruding as a reddened mass. It's not painful, but it is alarming looking, and the tear gland can be damaged unless it's taken care of. In the past this condition was treated by surgically removing the gland, but we now know that this gland is responsible for about one-third of the dog's tear production. Such surgeries predisposed dogs to dry eyes. Now treatment is to tuck the gland back in place and tack it down. It may have to be repeated. Cherry eye (technically, prolapsed gland of the nictitans) occurs in Cocker Spaniels much more often than in most other breeds. A mode of inheritance, if any, is unknown.

Dry-eye syndrome. This condition, more formally known as kerato-conjunctivitis sicca (KCS), occurs when the dog doesn't produce a normal amount of tears. The lack of tears causes the cornea, which is the outer clear coat of the eye, to dry out. The dog may blink, squint, and rub at his eyes. The eye becomes reddened, dull, and usually has a thick green or yellow mucus discharge. Left untreated, the eye often becomes infected, and the cornea can become cloudy and ulcerated, ultimately leading to blindness. This is a painful condition, and the dog may become lethargic as the pain increases.

Your veterinarian can diagnose the condition with a simple Schirmer tear test. It's done by placing a strip of special paper under the lower lid to measure how many tears are absorbed in one minute. If your Cocker has a mucus discharge or any other signs of KCS, you should have this inexpensive test performed.

More Cocker Spaniels are affected by this condition than any other breed of dog. Although several causes of KCS are known, the most

No Cocker's family tree is completely free of hereditary health disorders. The trick is making sure they don't cause disease in your dog's generation or beyond.

common is thought to be immune-mediated, in which an abnormal immune response attacks the tear glands. Its genetic component is unknown, although most researchers consider it hereditary.

In mild cases, artificial tear solutions such as those available over the counter for people can be instilled into the eye several times a day. Unfortunately, it's not usually

Healthy eyes are clear and without discharge, but you can't get the full story without a thorough veterinary ophthalmoscopic exam.

possible to keep to a schedule that allows the eye to remain sufficiently lubricated. Therapy with cyclosporine A is very often successful in treating dogs with immune-mediated KCS. For dogs that don't respond to drug therapy, a surgical option (called a parotid duct transposition) involving rerouting salivary ducts to the eye is often successful.

Imperforate lacrimal punctum. The tear glands constantly produce tears that wash over the surface of the eye and are then drained through the lacrimal ducts. It's very common that these lacrimal ducts fail to open in Cockers, so instead of draining properly the tears overflow from the inner corner of the eye and spill out onto the face. They can be surgically opened.

Glaucoma. The area between the cornea and the lens is filled with an aqueous fluid that constantly drains at the same rate as it is produced, thus maintaining a proper intraocular pressure (IOP). In some Cockers the drainage of fluid can't keep up with its production, so the fluid builds up within the eyeball and the IOP increases. If the pressure stays high for even a few hours, it can cause permanent damage and blindness.

Hereditary glaucoma is of three different types, of which two are seen in Cockers: narrow-angle and goniodysgenesis.

Most Cockers with glaucoma develop it between 5 and 8 years of age. Diagnosis is with a simple and inexpensive test your veterinarian can perform. Symptoms often appear suddenly, and include reddened eye, clouded cornea, enlarged pupil, squinting, tearing, pawing at the eye, hanging the head, and avoidance of light. This is an extremely painful condition, and warrants a trip to the emergency veterinarian if it occurs after hours. Even with immediate treatment, most eyes cannot be saved. When vision is lost, it's often best to remove the eye, since it can still be painful. At that point treatment is aimed at preventing the condition in the remaining eye. Even with such prevention, glaucoma in the second eye usually occurs within three years.

With treatment, an eye with a moderate rise in IOP can often be controlled, at least temporarily. Oral drugs and eyedrops may control the IOP and reduce the pain. Surgical options include using a laser to destroy the fluid-producing part of the eye, or redirecting the fluid into the eye socket by way of a small tube inserted into the eye.

Cataracts. The lens is the part of the eye situated behind the pupil. It's responsible for focusing light on the light-sensitive retina. Because the lens grows throughout life, it naturally becomes denser and somewhat cloudy with age. That's normal. However, in some dogs the lens becomes not just cloudy, but opaque, at an early age. The opacity, or cataract, can grow over weeks or years until it covers the entire lens and results in a dog that is essentially blind.

Fortunately, just as in humans, cataracts can be removed. A canine ophthalmologist will first test to make sure your Cocker's retina is functioning. It would be foolish to remove the lens and then discover the dog had a retina that didn't work, perhaps because of progressive retinal atrophy (see page 100). Assuming the retina is functioning, the lens will be removed and an artificial lens put in its place. Without the artificial lens, your dog could see, but everything would be way out of focus. This surgery has a high success rate.

When cataracts occur in anything but old dogs, they usually result from a hereditary condition. Cataracts are roughly divided according to age of onset. Cocker Spaniels appear to have more than one form of hereditary cataracts, classified as congeni-

Coping with a Blind Cocker

Dogs adjust surprisingly well to loss of vision, especially if it happens gradually. You can help by making pathways in your yard with stone or gravel walkways, or in your home with carpet or vinyl runners. You can also use scent and sound beacons so your dog can quickly orient toward your house or door. Don't rearrange furniture without guiding him through it several times. Walks should be on a leash.

tal, juvenile, or adult. The exact mode of genetic transmission isn't yet known, but it's suspected that the congenital form (present at birth) is inherited as an autosomal recessive, and the juvenile and adult forms either as autosomal recessives or polygenic traits.

Cocker Spaniels are among the breeds most often seen with cataracts. They commonly first appear in young adults and middle-aged dogs less than 8 years old, and usually both eyes are eventually affected.

Retinal dysplasia. This condition, also called retinal folds in its mild form, results when one or more layers of the retina fold during development, possibly causing blind spots in one or both eyes. It's present soon after birth, and is best detected by an ophthalmologist when the dog is 12 to 16 weeks of age. The condition in Cockers is usually mild, consisting of at most a few areas of folds that don't affect vision.

Progressive retinal atrophy (PRA). The retina is located at the back of the eye and contains the light-sensitive cells called rods and cones. PRA is a family of disorders that affects the retina, eventually leading to blindness. It's roughly analogous to the family of retinal disorders in people known as retinitis pigmentosa. Several forms are caused by various genes and result in various ages of onset. In Cockers, onset can range from as early as 18 months to as late as 7 years, but is most commonly seen between 3 and 6 years of age. A canine ophthalmologist can diagnose it earlier, usually by 12 to 18 months of age, with an electroretinography (ERG) test.

The condition is progressive and affects both eyes. Nothing can be done to prevent or slow it. It is not painful. Symptoms first appear as night blindness, with the dog often hesitant to go downstairs in dim light. It gradually progresses to day blindness, until the dog becomes completely blind. The pupil is dilated wider than normal in an attempt to let more light in, so you may notice a large pupil or an increased reflection from it even in bright light. Complete blindness is the end result.

The type of PRA in Cockers is the most widespread in dogs: progressive rod cone dysplasia (*prcd*). A DNA test for *prcd* is available for English Cocker Spaniels, and a similar test for American Cockers is nearing completion. Almost all forms of PRA, including *prcd*, are inherited as autosomal recessives.

Skin Disorders

Your Cocker's coat is part of what makes him so glorious. It's maddening when some skin disorder works to wreck it. Skin diseases usually can be managed, but they often take a large commitment to deal with effectively. Clipping the coat short will help during the treatment phase.

Allergies

If your Cocker is scratching, chewing, rubbing, and licking, he may have allergies. He may be allergic to inhaled allergens, things he comes in contact with, foods, or fleas. Unlike humans, where hay fever and other inhaled allergens typically cause sneezing, in dogs they more often cause itching. Food, too, can cause allergies. Signs of allergies are typically reddened, itchy skin, particularly around the ears, eyes, feet, forelegs, armpits, and abdomen. The dog may scratch and lick, and rub his face on furniture or rugs.

Allergens can be isolated with a test in which small amounts of allergen extracts are injected under the skin and are then monitored for reactions. Besides avoiding allergens, some treatments are available.

The most common inhaled allergens are dander, pollen, dust, and mold. They are often seasonal. Signs most commonly appear between 1 and 3 years of age. Treatment includes antihistamines, glucocorticoids, and hyposensitization.

The most common allergy among all dogs is flea allergy dermatitis (FAD), which is an allergic reaction to the saliva that a flea injects under the skin whenever it feeds. It causes intense itching not only in that area, but all over the dog, especially around the rump, legs, and paws.

DNA tests can be performed at any age.

Even a single flea bite can cause severe reactions in allergic dogs.

Seborrhea

Many Cockers are affected by seborrhea, a disorder in which the outer layer of the skin (the epidermis), the sebaceous glands, and part of the hair follicles have an increased rate of cell turnover. This results in excessive production of scale and sebum, which appear as dry flakes and greasy skin. Because the ear canals are lined with skin, seborrhea also affects them, causing waxy ear infections. In most affected Cockers, the greasy form of the disease predominates. The greasy skin smells bad and the hair may fall out when pulled.

The condition can be primary, which usually appears by 2 years of age and has a hereditary component, or secondary, which usually appears in older dogs as a response by the skin to other disorders. A

Those Cocker Ears

The Cocker's ear has several attributes that predispose it to problems. As in all dogs, its ear canal is made up of an initial vertical segment that abruptly turns inward at a sharp angle. The Cocker's canal is fairly long, sometimes with extra folds in it, both factors adding to its surface area and restricting the ability of air to flow freely through its length. The restricted airflow prevents moisture from evaporating and creates a warm, humid environment perfect for nurturing bacteria and fungus. Although certain types of bacteria are normal and harmless inhabitants of the ear canal, others can grow unchecked, causing the ear canal's surface to react to their by-products by secreting oils and becoming inflamed. The inflammation causes swelling, further restricting the flow of air.

Overzealous cleaning can actually contribute to the problem. A certain amount of wax is normal and serves a protective function in the ear. If you dig down with cotton swabs and scratch the delicate lining, you create a foothold for bacteria.

Other factors contribute to ear problems in Cockers, however. Seborrhea causes itchiness and contributes to a heavy accumulation of earwax. Allergies are the most common cause of ear problems in dogs overall. Parasites, such as ear mites, also can cause intense itching. Your veterinarian can prescribe much more effective medication for ear mites than you can buy over the counter.

Signs: Signs of ear problems can include head shaking, head tilt, scratching at the ear, rubbing the ear, smelly ear, and dark buildup within the ear. These same signs can occur no matter what the cause, yet the various causes require different treatments. In addition, in cases of chronic problems, the eardrum could be perforated, in which case you would not want to put the same medications into the ear as you would with an intact ear. For these reasons, ear problems should be examined by a veterinarian.

Treatment: If the problem is an infection, the veterinarian will prescribe ointment or drops that will kill fungus and bacteria. If the infection is advanced, oral antibiotics may also be prescribed.

If the ear is filled with wax and debris, it will need to be cleaned so the medication can reach the lining of the canal. If the ear is painful it will be impossible to clean it without sedating the dog. You also don't want to do this if the eardrum is perforated. In most cases, however, the veterinarian will also send you home with an ear-flush solution. Ear-flush solution not only loosens wax and debris so medication can reach the ear's surface, but has a drying agent so it doesn't leave the ear wet. Squirt the liquid in quickly (the slower it goes in the more it tickles) then gently massage it around the base of the ear. Let go and stand back while your dog shakes. Then do it again. After the ear is cleaned, you can squeeze medicated ointment or drops into the canal, again gently massaging the ear base to disperse the medicine.

Allowing air to reach the canals can be helpful in curing ear infections. You can hold the ears back by slipping a length of nylon stocking over the head with the ears folded back. You can even add holes in the stocking over the canals to aid in ventilation. You also can fasten the hair (not the leather) of the ears together so they are held back ponytail style. Shave the hair around the ear opening to allow maximal ventilation even when the ears are down. You may have to experiment to find something your Cocker will tolerate.

Unfortunately, treatment failure is common in Cockers. That's partly because the initial anatomy that caused the problem is unchanged, and when you quit giving the medicine the condition comes right back. The longer the condition persists, the more the skin lining the canal thickens, eventually becoming so scarred and thickened that it further occludes the canal.

Surgical correction: In chronic cases dogs can benefit from surgically removing some of the folds and thickened skin, allowing air to reach the canal more easily. If done early in the course of disease, a minimal amount of tissue will need to be removed. If you wait until the condition is advanced, more of the thickened tissue will need to be eliminated and the procedure will be more involved. The dog usually recovers rapidly and feels much better afterward.

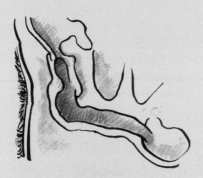 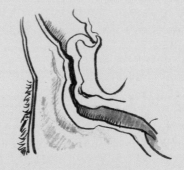

Cockers have slightly narrower ear canals than most other dogs. This, combined with several other traits, encourages ear infections.

severe form of seborrhea, called idiopathic seborrheic dermatitis, is seen almost exclusively in spaniels, especially Cockers. In these dogs the seborrhea leads to secondary infections from bacteria or yeast, which causes itching and skin lesions. Scratching further irritates the skin and spreads the infection.

A tentative diagnosis can be made visually, but a definite diagnosis requires a skin biopsy, which is done with local anesthetic. Any secondary infections must be cleared up before a diagnosis can be made.

Management is mostly through the use of antiseborrheic shampoos and moisturizers, with frequent bathing (two or three times a week) at first. The medicated shampoo must soak in for ten to fifteen minutes, and then be rinsed thoroughly to remove scales and grease. Following the bath with a moisturizer, as well as misting the coat with a dilute moisturizer, can help reduce itching. Bathing frequency usually can be reduced in time, and in fact, too much bathing can be counterproductive.

Some dogs fail to respond and may require drug therapy. Retinoic acid etretinate has been used with some success in Cockers. Other drugs have also had some success, but long-term use of them, as is usually required, may have unwanted side effects.

Vitamin A–Responsive Dermatitis

Cockers are one of a handful of breeds that occasionally have a condition in which scaling and crusting occur around the hair follicle, causing dandruff, crusting, and hair loss, especially along the back. A skin biopsy can provide a diagnosis. Treatment is with megadoses of vitamin A. These dogs are not nutritionally deficient in vitamin A, and in fact have normal blood levels of vitamin A. No evidence as to whether the disorder has a hereditary component is available.

Blood and Metabolic Disorders

If your Cocker doesn't have the vim and vigor you think he should, consider having your veterinarian test for metabolic diseases. Dogs can suffer from a variety of these as well as blood diseases. Some breeders believe immune-mediated hemolytic anemia, in which the dog's immune system turns against its own blood cells, is overrepresented in Cockers.

Hypothyroidism

Cocker Spaniels rank among the top breeds in which hypothyroidism is most commonly seen. Thyroid hormone affects metabolism, so when insufficient amounts are produced the dog can gain weight, become lethargic, become easily chilled, and shed skin and hair excessively. The skin may become thickened and dark.

Diagnosis is with one of several blood tests. The simplest is for baseline serum T4. If the test comes back in the middle or higher levels of normal range, the dog is normal. If it comes back low, however, additional testing is required before the dog should be labeled hypothyroid. More definitive tests are free T4 measured by equilibrium dialysis (FT4), canine thyroid stimulating hormone (cTSH), and thyroid autoantibody levels. The combination of FT4 and cTSH is a good screening tool for most dogs.

An important cause of hypothyroidism is autoimmune thyroiditis, in which the body's own immune system attacks the thyroid gland. A blood test for thyroglobulin autoantibody formation can detect the presence of the antibodies before clinical signs of hypothyroidism, usually by 3 to 4 years of age. Screening should begin at 2 years of age and be continued every year or other year through 8 years of age. The Orthopedic Foundation for Animals (OFA), and the American Spaniel Club maintain a registry for Cockers and other dogs that have been tested for autoimmune thyroiditis. Based on their statistics, Cockers are about the sixteenth most affected breed, with about 17 percent of Cockers in their registry positive for autoimmune thyroiditis. The condition is considered hereditary.

Treatment is with replacement hormone therapy. It takes several months for results to be noticeable, and dosage may often need to be adjusted.

Phosphofruktokinase Deficiency (PFK)

This is an autosomal recessive disease that interferes with the conversion of glucose to energy as well as the formation of red blood cells. It causes exercise intolerance, muscle cramping, and anemia. Signs may be evident as early as 3 months of age, but more often are not noticed until after a year. Affected dogs should not be allowed to tire themselves. No treatment is available, but some veterinarians advise supplementing with Co-Q-10, riboflavin, and L-Carnitine.

Many affected dogs are mildly anemic. Some have anemic crises, which may be identified by panting in the absence of heat, exertion, or obvious causes of stress, as well as by pale gums and often a brownish tinge to the urine. These cases require veterinary attention.

Metabolic disorders can interfere with your Cocker's ability to live life to its fullest.

It's estimated about 1 in 100 Cockers has PFK. Fortunately, a DNA test is available that can identify not only affected dogs, but also carriers. Affected dogs should not be bred, and carriers should not be bred to one another. The OFA maintains a registry of dogs that have been DNA-tested for PFK.

von Willebrand's Disease (vWD)

The most common hereditary bleeding disorder in dogs, vWD is caused by a deficiency in von Wille-brand factor. Although rare in Cockers, it does occur, resulting in moderate to severe bleeding. Several different types of vWD are found in various breeds; the exact type that Cockers have is not known. It is believed to be inherited as an incomplete dominant with variable penetrance. Diagnosis is with a blood test. DNA tests are available for several breeds, but at this writing not for Cockers. No preventive treatment is available, but severe bleeding episodes can be treated with blood transfusions.

Skeletal and Joint Problems

Joint problems make it difficult to jump for joy. Early diagnosis can sometimes help alleviate arthritic changes.

Hip Dysplasia

Hip dysplasia is a potentially crippling problem in which the head of the femur (thighbone) doesn't fit properly in the hip socket. The depth and shape of the socket may be a bad fit for the femur head and the joint may be lax. When pressure is put on the joint, such as when the dog walks, the femur pops in and out of place. Besides being painful, this further deteriorates the socket's rim, so the condition gets gradually worse, leading to degenerative joint disease. That's why early diagnosis is important.

Hip radiographs can detect hip dysplasia before outward signs are apparent. In the United States, radiographs are usually rated by either the Orthopedic Foundation for Animals (OFA) or the Pennsylvania Hip Improvement Program (PennHIP). The PennHIP method can detect changes earlier, but the OFA has the largest database. Both require the dog be anesthetized for the procedure.

The OFA rates radiographs according to the several specific joint characteristics. A dog with normal hips, which includes ratings of excellent, good, and fair, receives an OFA number. Dogs with borderline ratings should be rechecked in another six to eight months. Dysplastic hips include ratings of mild, moderate, and severe. The OFA statistics for Cockers show that about six percent of those in their registry overall are dysplastic, with three percent of those in the last decade dysplastic. About ten percent are rated as having excellent hips. That means most Cockers are probably somewhere in between. Hip dysplasia is considered to have a polygenic hereditary basis.

Mild cases of hip dysplasia may not need specific treatment, but more severe cases may need timely surgery to prevent crippling disability. Younger dogs that don't yet have arthritic changes can have a triple pelvic osteotomy (TPO), in which the orientation of the hip socket is changed to allow the femur head a better fit. Dogs with more advanced dysplasia may need a total hip replacement, in which the ball of the femur is replaced with a metallic ball and the socket is replaced with a Teflon cup. A third procedure that may be fine in a Cocker, especially an older or smaller one, is to simply remove the head of the femur. It's less expensive than the other surgeries, but not recommended for large or extremely active dogs.

Patellar Luxation

Patellar luxation is a common problem of smaller dogs in which the patella, or kneecap, of one or both rear legs slips out of position. Normally, the patella slides up and down

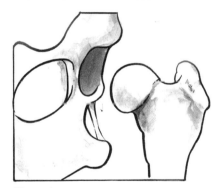

Normal

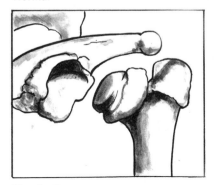

Dysplastic

Hip dysplasia.

Healthy joints help your Cocker run faster and jump higher.

in a small groove (the trochlear groove) of the femur (thighbone) as the knee moves. It's secured in that groove not only by the deepness of the groove but also by the tendon of the quadriceps muscle and by the joint capsule. In some dogs the groove is too shallow or the muscle exerts too much rotational pull, allowing the patella to ride over the ridge of the groove. Once out of place (luxated), the muscle must relax before it can pop back into place. Relaxing the muscle means the leg must be straightened at the knee, so the dog will often hop for a few steps with the leg held straight until the patella pops back into place. This hurts, so the dog may yelp. It also wears down the ridge, causing the condition to get gradually worse.

The condition may occur in one or both legs, and the patella may be displaced toward the outside of the leg or, more commonly, the inside (which can give a bowlegged appearance). Signs are usually apparent by 6 months of age. Early diagnosis is helpful in slowing the progress, but treatment depends on what the grade of severity is.

• Grade 1: The dog may occasionally skip, holding one hind leg forward for a step or two. The patella returns to its correct position easily.

• Grade 2: The dog often holds the affected leg up when moving, and the patella may not slide back into position by itself.

• Grade 3: The patella is usually out of position, slipping back out almost as soon as it is replaced. The dog only sometimes uses the affected leg.

• Grade 4: The patella is always out of position and cannot be replaced manually. The dog never puts weight on the leg.

If your Cocker has Grade 1 or 2 luxation, you may be able to slow the progress by keeping the dog's weight down, and keeping the muscle tone up with steady walking. Glucosamine supplements may help to build cartilage. Surgery to reconstruct the soft tissue surrounding the patella may prevent further progress if done early enough.

Grades 3 and 4 can be quite painful and cannot be treated conservatively. Surgery to tighten any stretched tissues and reconstruct the groove or realign the muscle will improve the condition, but may not return the leg to perfect. An orthopedic specialist has the best chance of success.

The OFA offers a registry for patellar luxation. Although only a limited number of Cocker Spaniels have been evaluated through the OFA, the data collected indicates that these dogs have the third-highest prevalence of all breeds, with 25 percent affected. This may be an overestimation, but it does indicate that the condition is a concern in the breed.

Intervertebral Disc Disease

Intervertebral disc disease is similar to the well-known problem in short-legged breeds and a few others, including Cocker Spaniels. The intervertebral discs are the cushions

Reading an OFA Number

A dog with normal hips receives an OFA number, such as CS1333G24M-PI, in which CS stands for Cocker Spaniel, 1333 means this is the 1,333rd Cocker to receive an OFA number, the G stands for good (it could also be F for fair or E for excellent), the 24 stands for the dog's age in months when X-rayed, the M stands for male (F for female), and the PI for permanent identification in the form of a tattoo or microchip (NOPI for no such identification).

between the spinal discs. The gelatinous substance in them is abnormally fibrous in some dogs and can become calcified, losing its elasticity. If too much force, especially twisting force, is applied to part of a disc, it can rupture and squeeze into the area surrounding the spinal cord, compressing the cord. Prevention entails guarding against undue stress on the discs by avoiding obesity and, in dogs that do appear to have a problem, avoiding jumping and twisting.

Signs of disc herniation depend on location and severity. They may range from a stiff, painful neck, to an arched back and stiff gait, to crying when lifted, a wobbly gait, toe dragging, and even rear end paralysis. Quick treatment with drugs to reduce swelling and strict, prolonged cage rest is essential. Surgery may be necessary to prevent irreversible spinal cord damage.

Screening for Cocker conditions lessens the possibility of heartaches from health problems.

Cocker Cardiomyopathy

Dilated cardiomyopathy (DCM) is a disease of the heart muscle in which it becomes thin and stretched until it can longer pump effectively. Several different kinds appear to exist in different breeds, with Cockers susceptible to an unusual type that appears to be associated with abnormally low levels of taurine.

If a Cocker Spaniel develops cardiomyopathy, he should be given supplemental taurine (500 mg twice a day) while awaiting the results of taurine levels in the blood. If taurine levels are low, the supplementation should continue. In that case, improvement should be noticed in three to four months. Although the condition is identified with Cocker Spaniels, it's not that common even in them. In fact, a Cocker has a greater chance of getting a heart problem such as mitral valve endocardiosis, common to many breeds.

Neural Diseases

The most widespread disease of the nervous system is epilepsy.

Epilepsy

Epilepsy, which refers to repeated seizures of unknown cause, is fairly common in many breeds, including Cockers. It appears to have a genetic component, but different genes are probably responsible for different forms of epilepsy in different breeds. That gene has not yet been found for the Cocker.

Seizures may be focal or generalized; the latter can be further divided into grand mal (convulsive) and petit mal (nonconvulsive). Generalized grand mal seizures are the type most often seen in dogs. They typically begin with the dog acting nervous, then exhibiting increasingly peculiar behaviors such as staring, trembling, salivating, or being unresponsive. This preictal stage is followed by the ictal stage, in which the dog will typically stiffen, fall over, paddle its legs, and champ its jaws, possibly also urinating, defecating, and vocalizing.

A seizing dog should be kept clear of dangers such as stairways and potential falling objects, and of other dogs, which often attack a convulsing dog. This ictal stage typically lasts a couple of minutes. The dog must be rushed to an emergency clinic if it continues for more than ten minutes because permanent brain damage or death from overheating can occur. The veterinarian will administer injections of Valium and phenobarbitol to stop the seizure.

After the ictal stage the dog will remain disoriented, may be temporarily blind, and will be exhausted. This may last from minutes to days. A veterinary exam should be performed as soon as possible. The vet-

erinarian will want to know details of the seizure, such as whether all the activity was on only one side.

Dogs with recurrent seizures may need medication. Phenobarbitol or, less commonly, potassium bromide, are given as a preventive. Your veterinarian may also prescribe Valium suppositories to have on hand in case of a seizure.

Do You Plan to Breed?

Breeding your dog may seem like a fun and profitable idea. Done right, it can be fun but is seldom profitable. Done wrong, it's neither. Without proper care, you won't be producing quality puppies. Without proper health testing, you could create puppies that will provide heartache to their families. Without proper preparation, you may not find families that provide suitable lifelong homes for your puppies. Without proper knowledge, you may not be able to cope with a whelping problem. Because the scope of information required is more than can be contained in one chapter here, you should consult a book specifically about breeding if you intend to take that step.

Recall what you looked for in a responsible breeder when you were searching for a puppy (see Chapter Three, Cocker Choices). If you can meet those criteria, you have the potential to become an asset to the breed.

Chapter Ten
Cocker Competitions

The Cocker Spaniel is a sporting dog, so sports come naturally to her. Although you'll find that the greatest pleasure of sharing your life with a Cocker are the everyday adventures, many Cocker owners also find it fun to show off their dogs and earn titles. It's a way of memorializing the time and effort you've spent with your dog, and of meeting other dog enthusiasts. Most Cockers find competition exhilarating. One of the joys of owning a Cocker is that she is good at just about everything.

The Cocker Good Citizen

You'll probably spend a good deal of time with your Cocker Spaniel in public. As such, you and she will represent Cockers and their owners to a wide segment of the population. If your dog barks and snaps, or throws herself on everyone she meets, she will give the breed a bad reputation, and just as important, the two of you

You know your Cocker is the best. Did you know there are many ways to prove it?

will miss out on a lot of opportunities you could have shared because you'd have to leave her at home.

As a Cocker owner, a major part of your training goals will be to have your dog control herself and behave in public. The American Kennel Club has outlined a series of exercises your dog should master to be a good public citizen. The club also offers a simple test where she can demonstrate her proficiency and earn the Canine Good Citizenship title. To earn the title she will be asked to

• Accept a friendly stranger without acting shy or resentful, or breaking position to approach; sit politely for petting and allow the stranger to examine her ears, feet, and coat, and to brush her.

• Walk politely on a loose leash, turning and stopping with you, walking through a group of at least three other people without jumping on them, pulling, or acting overly exuberant, shy, or resentful. She need not be perfectly aligned with you, but she shouldn't be pulling.

• Sit and lie down on command (you can gently guide her into position) and the stay as you walk 20 feet away and back.

• Stay and then come to you when called from 10 feet away.
• Behave politely to another dog and handler team, showing only casual interest in them.
• React calmly to distractions such as a dropped chair or passing jogger without panicking, barking, or acting aggressively.
• Remain calm when held by a stranger while you're out of sight for three minutes.
• Refrain from eliminating, growling, snapping, biting, or attempting to attack a person or dog throughout the evaluation.

All the tests are done on lead; a long line is provided for the Stay and Recall exercises. The Canine Good Citizenship title is one of the most important ones your dog can earn.

Mind Games

How smart is your spaniel? Smart enough to heel, sit, lie down, come, and stay when told? If so, she has the makings of an obedience title holder. Cockers are naturals for obedience work. Their affinity for being at your side makes them willing heelers, their inclination to freeze makes them better able to stay when told, and their hunting heritage makes them natural-born retrievers. Overlay their merry disposition, and you have a dog that performs an obedience routine with flair. Of course, they also don't mind adding in their own interpretation once in a while, which often lends a comedic aspect to the whole affair.

You plan to teach your Cocker the basics of sitting, heeling, staying, and coming, and perhaps getting a Canine Good Citizenship title. It's a small step to earn a Rally obedience title from there, or perhaps a traditional obedience title.

Rally

Rally obedience is more casual that traditional obedience. In rally, you and your dog walk a predetermined course along which numbered signs are placed. Each sign will direct you to have your dog do something, such as sit, circle to the left, do a figure eight, about-turn, or for you to leave and then call your dog. The exact exercises and their sequence vary from trial to trial. You can repeat commands, praise your dog, and pretty much act as you would normally except that you can't touch her. Precision is not an important part of rally obedience. Rally has three different degrees of difficulty.

Rally Novice class is judged with the dog always on a leash. It consists of ten to fifteen stations (signs) with no more than five stationary exercises. A dog that passes three times earns the Rally Novice (RN) title. Examples of exercises include serpentine weave, down from a walk, moving side step to the right, circle, and spiral.

Rally Advanced class is judged with the dog always off the leash. It consists of twelve to seventeen stations with no more than seven stationary exercises. A dog that passes three times earns the Rally Advanced

(RA) title. Examples of exercises in addition to those in the Novice class are send-over jump, various pivots, and call to heel position.

Rally Excellent class is judged with the dog always off leash except for the Honor exercise. It consists of fifteen to twenty stations with no more than seven stationary exercises. A dog that passes three times earns the Rally Excellent (RE) title. Examples of exercises in addition to the Novice exercises are back up three steps, halt-stand-down sequence, and honoring, in which a dog stays in the ring while another dog performs its exercises.

Rally Advanced Excellent (RAE) title is earned by qualifying ten times in both Advanced and Excellent at the same trial.

Obedience

Rally obedience is a fun way to enter the world of dog obedience. If you and your dog are more the precision types, though, you may prefer traditional obedience. In these trials you can't talk or gesture to your dog except to give commands, and can praise only between exercises. Instead of following printed directions, a judge tells you what to do as you go along. You get few, if any, second chances, and precision counts.

Novice Obedience class consists of
• Heeling on and off the leash, with the dog sitting automatically each time you stop; negotiating right, left, and about-turns; and changing to a faster and slower pace.

Advanced obedience levels include retrieving a dumbbell.

• Heeling on a leash in a figure eight around two people.
• Standing off lead without moving while the judge touches the dog.
• Waiting for you to call and then coming from about 20 feet (about 6 m) away, and then returning to heel position on command.
• Staying in a sit position for one minute, and then a down position for three minutes, in a group of other dogs while you are 20 feet (about 6 m) away.

If your dog passes three times, she earns the Companion Dog (CD) title.

Open Obedience class consists of
• Heeling, including a figure eight, off the leash.
• Coming when called as in Novice, except dropping to a down position

when told to do so about halfway back to you, and then continuing the recall when commanded.
• Retrieving a thrown dumbbell first over flat ground and then over a jump.
• Jumping over a broad jump.
• Staying in a sit position for three minutes, and then a down position for five minutes, in a group of other dogs while you are out of view.

If your dog passes three times, she earns the Companion Dog Excellent (CDX) title.

Utility Obedience class consists of
• Heeling, coming, standing, sitting, downing, and staying in response to hand signals.
• Allowing the judge to touch her while the handler is 10 feet (3 m) away.
• Retrieving a leather, and then a metal, article scented by the handler from a group of similar unscented articles.
• Retrieving one of three gloves designated by the handler.

• Trotting away from the handler until told to stop and turn around 40 feet (12 m) away, and then jumping the designated jump and returning to the handler. This is then repeated, jumping the opposite jump.

If your dog passes three times, she earns the Utility Dog (UD) title.

Utility Dog Excellent (UDX) title is awarded for qualifying in both Open and Utility classes on the same day at ten trials.

Obedience Trial Champion (OTCH) is the supreme obedience title, requiring a dog earn 100 points, plus three first placements, by scoring better than other qualifying dogs in Open or Utility. At this writing, eleven Cockers have achieved this highest honor.

High in Trial (HIT) is awarded to the top scorer of the day at an obedience trial.

On the Trail

How many times have you taken your Cocker for a walk to some exotic location you were sure she'd enjoy, only to have her spend the entire time sniffing the grass? She is enjoying it, in her own way. While you marvel at the vista of the Grand Canyon, she's found something equally fascinating in the trail of a deer that has recently passed. She's sniffing the air for the scent of a bird hiding in the brush, or checking out another dog's calling card. She's wondering what your problem is that you don't find these equally enthralling, and she's right. You are the one lacking in olfactory ability, the one essentially odor blind.

Your Cocker Spaniel, like all dogs, has a sense of smell that is so acute that we cannot even comprehend what her world must be like. Why not put it to the test? You can train her to use her nose to track people or find lost objects. The AKC awards several titles to dogs that prove their ability to track.

But how do dogs trail? They probably use a combination of factors. First, wherever you go, you are constantly leaving a trail of microscopic traces of skin, sweat, exhaled air, and perfumes or soaps. These float in the air and gradually settle to the earth. The dog's sensitive nose can detect them, either in the air or on the ground. Second, wherever you go you disturb what you're walking on. You stir up dirt and crush vegetation. Your dog's nose can also detect those odors. That's why some surfaces are easier to track on than others; slick, clean surfaces don't have much to be stirred up or to catch odor molecules, so they tend to be more difficult than rough, grassy surfaces. A certain amount of moisture, such as dew, also helps, but rain tends to disperse odors too much. These factors are why many people choose to train their dogs to track early in the morning, when the dew is still on the grass. You can also see your own tracks then, and can tell if your dog is on the right track.

If your dog is motivated by food, you can start by walking a short dis-tance (without your dog) and dropping a treat every few feet. Then go back and start him at the beginning of your trail, keeping him on-lead and letting him discover and eat the treats. As he catches on to this game, you can make the treats farther apart, so he will gradually figure out that he can find them by following your scent trail. Be sure you're not laying scent trails that are close to one another or cross one another. You want to keep it simple and make sure he always succeeds.

Another popular technique for dogs who are motivated more by a desire to be with you is to have a helper hold your dog while you walk away and hide. The helper then lets the dog find you. You gradually make more and more of your trail out of your dog's sight so he has to rely on his nose to discover you.

Eventually you will increase the distances and add turns to your trails. Then you may wish to fine-tune and get ready to earn one of the AKC tracking titles.
• *The Tracking Dog* (TD) title is earned by following a 440- to 500-yard (about 400 to 460 m) track with three to five turns laid by a person from thirty minutes to two hours beforehand.
• *The Tracking Dog Excellent* (TDX) title is earned by following an 800- to 1,000-yard (about 730–900 m) track with five to seven turns laid by a person from three to five hours before-hand. It may cross over varied terrain, such as plowed surfaces, bridges, and even slightly traveled

A Cocker hurdles a jump in an agility trial.

roads. The dog must also ignore a cross track laid shortly after the first track.

• *The Variable Surface Tracking* (VST) title is earned by following a 600- to 800-yard (about 550–730 m) track with three to five turns laid by a person from thirty minutes to two hours beforehand. The trail leads over at least three different types of surfaces, at least one of which must be vegetated and at least two of which must be nonvegetated, such as sand or concrete. The trail can lead through buildings, and may be crossed by animal, pedestrian, or vehicular traffic.

• *The Champion Tracker* (CT) title is awarded to dogs that earn all three tracking titles. More than 100 Cockers have earned TD titles and at least 20 have earned TDX titles. As of this writing, none has yet achieved the CT honor.

The Agile Cocker

For a pure adrenaline rush, few canine sports can beat agility. It's an obstacle course for dogs run against the clock, combining jumping, climbing, weaving, running, zipping through tunnels, and loads of fun! Cockers love it.

Several organizations, including the AKC, the United Kennel Club (UKC), the North American Dog Agility Council (NADAC), and the United States Dog Agility Association (USDAA) sponsor trials and award titles, each with slightly different fla-

Agile Cockers

The third dog of any breed, and the first Cocker, to earn the Master Agility Champion title is MACH2 Patriot Piper Cub VCD2, UDT. The VCD title is a versatility title. Once dogs accumulate enough points to earn the MACH, they can earn more points toward a MACH2, and so on. The highest Cocker MACH is MACH 8 Bar-Bax's Makin New Waves CD.

How many titles can one dog earn? Ask MACH ADCH NATCH/ATCH Rocko's Modern Life CGC PD1 GCH RCH-Bronze JCH-Silver TM-Silver SCH-Silver SaCH-Gold S-EAC S-EJC O-EGC O-TG-E O-TN-E O-WV-E O-Elite Versatility.

Other agility organizations award titles every bit as prestigious as the MACH. The USDAA awards the Agility Dog Champion (ADCH) title, which has been achieved by only eight Cockers, first by one named Chadwick. The only Cocker to achieve the coveted ADCH-Bronze designation is NATCH Brookwood Mad About You MX MXJ, TM-Gold.

MACH Mamaradlo's Midnight Beauty is the Cocker holder of the 60 Weave Pole Challenge, weaving between 60 poles in a mere 18.45 seconds.

vors of agility. The AKC program will be described here, but don't discount the others, which many competitors find to be even more fun.

The AKC obstacles:

- The A-frame is made of two boards 8 or 9 feet (2.4 or 2.7 m) long each and 3 to 4 feet (about 1 m) wide leaned against each other so they form an A-frame with the peak 5 to 5½ feet (1.5 to 1.7 m) off the ground. The dog runs up one side and down the other.
- The Dog Walk is a board 8 or 12 feet (2.4 or 3.6 m) long and 1 foot (30 cm) wide that is either 3 or 4 feet high, suspended between two like boards that lead up to it on one side and down from it on the other. The dog runs up one plank, over the horizontal plank, and down the other plank.
- The Teeter is a seesaw with a 12-foot (3.6 m) plank. The dog runs up one side until her weight causes the teeter to shift so she can walk down the other side.
- The Pause Table is about 3 feet (about 1 m) square. The dog has to jump up on it, then either sit or lie down as commanded for five seconds.
- The Open Tunnel is a flexible tube 10 to 20 feet (3–6 m) in length and about 2 feet (61 cm) in diameter. It is often bent into an S or C shape for the dog to run through.
- The Chute is a rigid barrel with a lightweight fabric chute about 12 to 15 feet (3.6 to 4.6 m) long attached to one end. The dog runs into the open end of the barrel and continues blindly through the collapsed chute until she comes out the other end.
- The Weave Poles area consists of 6 to 12 vertical poles spaced 20 to 24 inches (51–61 cm) apart. The dog takes a serpentine route, weaving

from one side of the poles to the other.

• The Jumps consist of single-bar, panel, double-bar, and triple-bar jumps. The double and triples are both wide and tall. The bars are easily displaced, making it safe when a dog fails to clear them. The dog must jump without knocking any bars down.

• The Tire Jump is about 2 feet (61 cm) in diameter with the bottom of the opening at the same height as the other jumps. The dog must jump through the opening.

• The Broad Jump is a spaced series of four to five slightly raised boards.

AKC Classes. AKC agility is divided into two types of courses. The Standard course comprises all the obstacle types, including those referred to as contact obstacles: the A-frame, dog walk, teeter, and pause table. The Jumpers with Weaves (JWW) course includes only jumps, tunnels, and weaves, usually in a somewhat more intricate pattern than the standard.

The Novice standard class uses 12 to 13 obstacles, and the Novice JWW class uses 13 to 15 obstacles. Dogs that qualify three times earn the Novice Agility (NA) or Novice Agility Jumpers (NAJ) titles, respectively.

The Open standard class uses 15 to 17 obstacles, and the Open JWW class uses 16 to 18 obstacles. Dogs that qualify three times earn the Open Agility (OA) or Open Agility Jumper (OAJ) titles, respectively.

Both Excellent standard classes use 18 to 20 obstacles. Dogs that qualify three times earn the Agility Excellent (AX) or Agility Excellent Jumpers (AXJ) titles. Dogs that continue to compete in Excellent, and earn 10 additional qualifying scores by finishing the course in a slightly shorter time than required for the AX and AXJ titles, earn the Master Agility (MA) and Master Agility Jumpers (MAJ) titles.

The Master Agility Champion (MACH) title is earned by qualifying at 20 trials in both Standard and Jumpers Excellent classes, and earning 750 points. One point is earned for each second under the allotted course time the dog completes the course in.

Naturally, not all dogs jump the same heights. Depending on their height, Cockers will compete in the 12-inch (for dogs less than 14 inches at the withers) or 16-inch (for dogs under 18 inches) divisions. If this seems too high for your dog you can enter the Preferred classes, which have lower jump heights. Titles earned in these classes are the same as regular titles but end in a "P."

The courses get tougher as the class level advances, so you will have to switch which side of the dog you're on, perhaps leading out from the start so she doesn't get ahead of you, and directing her to take an obstacle that is not the one directly in her path—all while the allotted times get shorter and shorter and the errors allowed decrease as the class level goes up.

Agility requires true teamwork and an athletic dog. It's not something you can force dogs to do; they will do it only if they love it. Fortunately, most Cockers love it. The combination of running, jumping, and making split-second decisions is exciting. A short agility session is enough to exercise both the body and mind.

You can start training at home with some low jumps. Practice having your dog work from both your left and right sides. You can entice her to walk through a short chute made of a sheet draped between some chairs. You can place some poles in the ground and start teaching her to weave. One way to do this is by placing the poles and then slanting every other one outward in the opposite direction, then walking your dog through the middle. Gradually straighten the poles so she has to start weaving to walk between them. Another way to do this is to offset every other pole so there is a channel between them, and then gradually move them closer to a single center line. Again, she will gradually have to start weaving to walk down the line. Your best bet, however, is to find an agility class. A good place to search for one, as well as everything agility, is through *www.cleanrun.com*.

Flyball!

Flyball is one of the few dog activities that is actually a team sport. It's a relay race in which each team member runs and jumps over a series of low hurdles, steps on a platform to release a ball, catches the ball, and returns so the next dog on the team can start. It's one of dog-

Flyball Titles

Dogs earn points toward flyball titles based on their team's time:
• less than 32 secs: each dog receives 1 point
• less than 28 secs: each dog receives 5 points
• less than 24 secs: each dog receives 25 points

Dogs can earn titles with the following points: 20 points—Flyball Dog (FD); 100 points—Flyball Dog Excellent (FDX); 500 points—Flyball Dog Champion (FDCh); 5,000 points—Flyball Master (FM); 10,000 points—Flyball Master Excellent (FMX); 15,000 points—Flyball Master Champion (FMCh); 20,000 points—Onyx Award; 30,000 points—Flyball Grand Champion (FGDCH).

Kake's Jazz Tri-Umph was the breed's first Flyball Grand Champion, earning 30,000 points in 1998.

dom's most frenetic activities. If you thrive on excitement and team play, flyball may be for you.

It sounds complicated to teach your dog to do all this, but it's not if you break it down into steps. First, your dog needs to learn to jump the hurdles. Start with three or four low hurdles, just 6 inches or so high. Place a barrier, such a temporary fencing, to create a chute so the dog has to jump to get to the other end. Leave your dog with a helper, then go to the other end of the chute and call her, running away and rewarding

Catch!

her with a toy or treat when she gets there. You want to encourage her to go fast! Eventually you will just make barriers next to the each hurdle, and then remove them altogether.

She also needs to know how to step on the platform. Place a nonslip surface at an angle and have her practice walking up and onto it, turning while on it, and walking off. You want her to place all four feet on it. Eventually you will encourage her to go faster.

Finally, you want her to learn to take a ball off the top of the platform. Eventually she will be getting it from the ball launcher. At this point you need to find a club to practice with, but you will have great head start!

Don't forget the noncompetitive sports you can do with your Cocker. Hiking, swimming, and going on trips can earn your dog the Best Companion award, the one that really counts because it's the one you'll give her.

Chapter Eleven
The Sporting Spaniel

"**S**paniels are flushing breeds. Their purpose is to hunt, find game, flush and retrieve birds in a pleasing and efficient manner." That's what the AKC says about spaniels in the field, and it's what your Cocker would love to have the chance to show you.

Spaniels are the do-it-all dog of the hunting world. Whereas most sporting breeds specialize in finding or retrieving game, spaniels help with every step. They start by searching for birds, quartering—that is, quickly moving back and forth in an arc about 20 to 30 feet or so in front of the handler—looking, listening, but mostly sniffing, for birds.

Once a bird is located, the dog flushes it by springing toward it so it takes flight. If he stops and points, some running birds can simply run away while he's just standing there. The hunter wants him to flush the bird so it can be shot. Ideally, once the bird takes flight the dog stops and tracks the flight so he can mark the bird's fall should the hunter shoot it. Then he waits for the hunter to send him to retrieve the bird. Waiting is an essential safety measure; a dog that continues to jump after a fly-

ing bird, or one that runs out to get a downed bird, risks getting shot. Once sent to retrieve, the spaniel may have to search for birds that have fallen in deep cover, or even water. He may even have to bring back wounded birds.

The Cocker's hunting ability is a combination of inborn tendencies and careful training. Although developed and used as an upland game hunter for generations, few Cockers today have any close ancestors that have been used for hunting Nonetheless, renewed interest in the Cocker as a hunting dog has led many Cocker owners to discover their dogs' hidden talents.

Field Training Your Cocker

You might think the best way to train your Cocker to hunt is to take him into the field and start finding birds. That might be a lot of fun, but it's not the way to create a reliable hunting companion. The best place to start training for the field is in your backyard, and the best thing to prac-

Cocker Spaniels are undergoing a revival of sorts when it comes to hunting.

tice with is a bird's wing attached to a long pole by an equal length of string. You'll also need a canvas-covered retrieving dummy (you can use a boat bumper in a pinch) and a spaniel whistle. A spaniel whistle is not as loud as a retriever whistle because it is generally used at closer range. Eventually you'll add live pigeons to your training arsenal, but for now you can also manage with commercially available bird scent.

Before starting, review the basic rules of training in Chapter Eleven, page 123. The concepts of field training are the same.

Birdiness

You can create interest in birds in a Cocker of any age by tying a bird wing onto one of your retrieving dummies (or for a young puppy, just use a soft toy, a knotted-up sock, or a clean fuzzy paint roller) and throwing it for him. You can practice this inside in a long hallway. Sit in the middle, throw toward one end, and when your dog brings it back, take it from him, praise, and throw another one to the other end. The main idea is to keep him excited, even if you have to go with him to get it, and to praise him for doing such a good job. If he still doesn't get it, hang it from a pole and let it dance around above him, or let it scurry along the ground. Adding bird scent will also help increase interest.

Don't let him chew on it, or play tug o'war with it, or play keep-away with it. If you have to train outside, you may need to keep a long leash on your dog so he can't take his prize and run off—definitely not desirable behavior in the field! If he tends to bite down too hard, practice using a rough scrub brush that won't feel so good to munch on. His training items are just for training; put them away when you are through.

Once your dog is interested in the bird wing, let him see you hide it and then let him go search it out for you. Once he knows the game, start telling him to "find it," and then start hiding it when he can't see you doing so. Now bring him back into the area (and you can even do this indoors), tell him to find it, and praise him when he sniffs it out.

As he gets more proficient, start demanding more. Reward him for delivering the item to your hand rather than just dropping it near you. Use a variety of items of different sizes, weights, and textures. You

Common Hunting Commands

- Verbal:
  Close: hunt close
  Fetch: retrieve
  Whoa: stop
  Come around: turn toward you
  Hup: stop or sit
  Hie on: send to start hunting
- Whistle:
  One sharp tweet: stop
  One long trill: come
  Two short tweets: turn or come around

You can teach voice and whistle commands at the same time, or teach whistle commands later by giving the whistle signal immediately followed by the voice signal.

Dummy birds are often used in demonstrations.

Cocker Coats in the Field

Cockers today have a much longer coat than they did when they were first developed for hunting. A long coat can pick up burrs and stickers, sometimes to the point of practically tying the dog's legs together. It can also create hours of grooming for you after each outing. Depending on your Cocker's coat and the type of terrain and growth where he will be hunting, you may find it easier to clip his coat short.

may consider teaching him a force retrieve, which he is taught he must do no matter what else catches his fancy. Several force retrieve methods exist, and most can be found in books dealing exclusively with training hunting spaniels and retrievers.

Of course, your dog will be using whole birds, not wings, when hunting. Most trainers advocate using dead pigeons for initial training. You can usually find these by contacting a bird-dog trainer in your area, or ask at a hunting supply store. You can freeze it, partially thaw it for training, then refreeze it for future use. A fully frozen bird isn't birdy-smelling enough. A partially thawed bird has a good scent but also a frozen core that is resistant and unappealing to bite into.

Introduce him to the dead bird much as you did to the bird wing, tantalizing him with it and then throwing it. Encourage him to retrieve it, and when he does, make a big deal out of the wondrous thing he has done. He may race around and refuse to give up such a grand prize. If he does so, take a step backward and practice relinquishing the wing.

The next step is to graduate to a live bird. Anyone who uses live birds for training must care for and handle them in the most humane way possible. The bird will have to be prevented from flapping and flying, either by pulling out the flight feathers on one wing or by covering the wing in a nylon stocking. Obviously if you pull the feathers you cannot just let the bird go afterward.

Once the bird cannot fly, place it on the ground and encourage your dog to retrieve it. This should be attempted only once your dog has proven he has a soft mouth when retrieving dead birds. Even so, you must be alert to stop him from biting down on or hurting the bird. After this step you can plant, or hide, the bird under cover, encouraging him to find and retrieve it. Plant the bird so that it is upwind from the dog, and be sure it has plenty of scent on the surrounding foliage.

Gunshots

A gun-shy Cocker isn't going to be much of a hunting partner. Start by introducing him to fairly quiet but sudden noises, each time following the noise with a treat or chance to retrieve. If he acts uneasy, try something a little less noisy, but don't coddle or berate him.

As he gets older, introduce louder noises by having a helper fire a cap

Retrieving to hand is required to earn higher-level field titles.

gun, then a .22 caliber blank pistol at a good distance from him, again feeding or throwing something for him immediately afterward. Your helper can gradually move closer and move up to a higher caliber gun as your dog comes to ignore the shots.

Quartering

Your Cocker's natural hunting style is quartering, but you can help him better master it with some training. He should already know the commands to go find it (or "hie on" as many hunters use) and come, preferably to the whistle.

Walk in a straight line, then say "hie-on!" and wave your arm to the right, angling right as you do and continuing to walk. If he's like most Cockers, he will run ahead of you, eager to lead the way. After he gets

about 20 yards ahead, tweet your whistle twice for him to come and turn to walk in the opposite direction. He should rush to catch up. Keep on, repeating the hand waving to go to the right and to the left, and then turning to go in the other direction. Eventually your goal is to turn your own body less and less while still signaling with your arm for your dog to angle out in one direction and then the other.

Once he has the hang of quartering, plant a bird upwind in the field. Walk toward it with him quartering in front of you. His job as a spaniel is not to point, but to rush in and flush the bird. If he starts to point, encourage him to rush in, even running along with him, so the bird attempts to flu up and he is rewarded by the excitement as well as your praise. If

he can't find the planted bird, keep on walking and then turn and walk toward it from another direction until he does. The more practice he gets finding birds when quartering, the sooner he will figure out that he is quartering for a reason, and he'll be ready to try out in the field on naturally occurring birds.

You may eventually wish to teach him to sit and wait once the bird is flushed. This makes it safer to hunt with him, and is a requirement at field trials and advanced levels of hunting tests.

Water Retrieving

Although Cockers are not water spaniels, there's always the possibility that a shot bird will fall in a pond or river. Rather than let it float away, the responsible hunter uses a dog to retrieve it. That's why it's important to teach your Cocker a water retrieve,

and why it's a requirement for earning most Cocker hunting and field titles.

Many Cockers are natural water dogs, but they still profit from early experience with water. You can start young puppies at home just by supplying a wading pool for them to play in, gradually adding more water. Throw treats and toys in it and encourage your dog to splash. Swimming pools are difficult to teach dogs in because their sudden drop-off intimidates them. Far better is a natural body of water with a gradual slope so he can get used to going deeper more slowly. It helps to have another water-savvy dog along, or you can get into the water, too. It also helps if your dog already knows how to retrieve; you can throw the retrieving dummy at an angle over the water, gradually throwing it farther out. Never throw it way out before he is an experienced swimmer. Then progress to dead birds.

Working Certificate Tests

After working with your Cocker you may be perfectly content to enjoy him all to yourself and just go hunting. But you may also be tempted to show the rest of the world what Cockers, and your Cocker in particular, can do. A range of tests and trials requiring various levels of proficiency are available for Cocker Spaniels. A test is a noncompetitive event in which a dog qualifies by meeting certain performance criteria. A trial, in comparison, is a competitive event in which a dog earns points or titles only by besting other dogs. The basics of the various tests and trials are outlined here. Consult the actual rules.

The American Spaniel Club offers a Working Certificate Test Program in which spaniels can earn noncompetitive titles by demonstrating their proficiency as hunting companions. The Working Dog (WD) certificate is awarded for satisfactory performance in all categories, and the Working Dog Excellent (WDX) for outstanding performance in all categories. A dog that damages a bird is considered an unacceptable hunting companion or field event competitor and cannot earn either certificate.

Test Procedure

Each dog should work at least two live birds (pigeon, quail, chukar, or pheasant) on land. Birds should be planted at least 20 to 30 yards ahead of the starting line and apart from each other. The unleashed dog must stay by the handler at the starting line until the handler sends the dog ahead. The dog works the field alone, with the hunter directing him when needed. The dog is expected to quarter the field in a workmanlike manner within gun range, displaying scenting ability and use of wind. Barking while quartering is penalized. The dog should show a reasonable response to a whistle or command. He should demonstrate a

desire to find and flush game without undue urging. The dog need not be steady to the flush or shot. For the WDX the dog must mark (that is, note the position of) a downed bird. For the WD the handler can direct the dog to the bird's fall. The dog is expected to retrieve a downed bird and deliver it to hand (for the WDX) or within a few steps of the handler (for the WD), in either case without chewing or damaging the bird.

For the water test a shot is fired and a dead bird is thrown about 10 to 15 yards into the water. The dog must swim and retrieve the bird to shore. For the WDX, the bird must be delivered to hand. A dog that must be coaxed to enter the water cannot receive a WDX. The dog cannot show gun-shyness for any test.

AKC Hunt Tests

The AKC offers Hunt Tests that are very similar to the Working Tests of the ASC. Dogs are judged in the following categories:

1. Hunting Ability (which includes desire, courage, perseverance, independence, and intelligence).

2. Bird-Finding Ability (which includes bird sense, response to wind and scenting conditions, and use of nose).

3. Flushing Ability (boldness).

4. Trained Abilities (which include range, pattern, gun response, and response to commands).

5. Retrieving Ability (which includes marking, enthusiasm, and mouth).

Each of these five categories is graded on a scale of 0 to10. A dog must earn at least a 5 in each category, with an overall average score of at least 7 to qualify.

For the Junior Hunter (JH) title, a dog must qualify in four separate tests. If a dog is already a JH, he needs to qualify at the Senior Hunter (SH) level at four events; to earn the SH title if he is *not* already a JH he must qualify at five such events. The Master Hunter (MH) title requires qualifying scores at six Hunt Tests unless the dog is already an SH, in which case he needs only five qualifying scores.

Junior Hunt Test

The Junior Hunter must find, flush, and retrieve two birds on land, and retrieve one bird from water at a distance of approximately 20 yards with a shot fired. He need not be steady to wing and shot, but should show no fear of cover. He should have a reasonable response to commands and maintain a reasonable working distance from the handler. Birds need not be delivered to hand, but must be delivered in close proximity to the handler.

Senior Hunt Test

The Senior Hunter must find, flush, and retrieve two birds to hand on land. When searching, the Senior Hunter should cover ground briskly and efficiently, addressing places birds are likely to be. He should hunt independently, without relying on cues from the handler, and should boldly enter cover or other difficult spots that could hold birds. He must also line steady (not physically held at the line) at water and retrieve one bird to hand from water at a distance of approximately 30 yards with a shot fired. He should be able to "hunt dead" (find a dead bird when the hunter knows only the general area the bird is in and the dog has not seen it fall or heard a gunshot) on a land blind of approximately 20 yards' distance. The dog need not be steady to wing and shot on land but should not show uncontrollable chasing in a missed bird situation.

Master Hunt Test

In addition to the requirements for a Senior Hunter, a Master Hunter must perform a blind water retrieve at a distance of approximately 30 yards, and must "hunt dead" on a land blind of approximately 40 yards' distance. He must be steady to wing

Field Firsts

The first Junior Hunter Cocker was Lynndale's Mr Deuteronomy CDX, WDX, JH; the first Senior Hunter was Deidree Shannon Dodge UDT, WDX, SH; and the first Master Hunter was CH Pett's Southwest Breeze CD WDX MH. Only a handful of Cockers have earned the MH title.

The first American Cocker Spaniel to win a Field Trial Championship since the 1960s was FC Madison's Pride and Passion SH.

"Where's that bird?"

and shot. He must give a finished performance and be easily under control at all times. Intelligent use of the wind and terrain in locating game, accurate nose, and intensity are essential.

AKC Field Trials

Field trials differ from hunting tests in that they are competitive events in which dogs compete against each other rather than simply meet a standard of satisfactory performance. Not only must a dog meet those standard requirements; he must excel at them by besting other dogs to gain his title. Field trial competitors should be able to do the work of a Master Hunter, but do it in an even more polished manner. Judges consider the following specific criteria:

• Control at all times, and under all conditions.
• Scenting ability and use of wind.
• Manner of covering ground and briskness of questing.
• Perseverance and courage in facing cover.
• Steadiness to flush, shot, and command.

Tip
If you attend a field trial, be sure to wear a blaze orange vest or hat, as it is required by the AKC.

- Aptitude in marking fall of game and ability to find it.
- Ability and willingness to take hand signals.
- Promptness and style of retrieve and delivery.
- Proof of tender mouth.

Spaniel field trials offer the following stakes:

- *Puppy:* For dogs under 2 years of age.
- *Novice:* For dogs that have never won first, second, third, or fourth in an Open All-Age Stake, a Qualified Open All-Age or an Amateur All-Age Stake, or first in any other regular stake (Puppy Stake excepted).
- *Novice Handler:* For Novice dogs handled by someone who has never handled a dog placed first, second, third, or fourth in an Open All-Age Stake, a Qualified Open All-Age Stake, or an Amateur All-Age Stake, or placed first in any other regular stake (Puppy Stake excepted).
- *Limited:* For dogs that have never won first place in an Open All-Age Stake, or two firsts in any regular official stake (Puppy Stake excepted).
- *Open All-Age:* For all dogs over 6 months of age.
- *Qualified Open All-Age:* For dogs over 6 months of age that have placed first, second, third, or fourth in any stake (Puppy Stake excepted).
- *Amateur All-Age:* For dogs over 6 months of age that are handled by amateurs. An amateur is somebody who has not accepted compensation for training or handling any breed of hunting dog in the field for a period of one year.
- *National Championship* for Cocker Spaniels (including English Cocker Spaniels): An annual event open only to certain qualifying dogs. The winner is designated the National Cocker Spaniel or English Cocker Spaniel Field Champion of that year.
- *National Amateur Championship* for Cocker Spaniels (including English Cocker Spaniels): An annual event open only to certain qualifying amateur-handled dogs. The winner is designated the National Amateur Cocker Spaniel or English Cocker Spaniel Field Champion of that year.

To become a Field Champion, a Cocker Spaniel must win either a National Championship Stake, two Open All-Age Stakes, two Qualified Open All-Age Stakes, or one Open All-Age Stake and one Qualified Open All-Age Stake at different trials with at least ten starters in either stake; or win one Open All-Age Stake or one Qualified Open All-Age Stake and 10 Championship points, which dogs accumulate by placing in Open All-Age or Qualified Open All-Age Stakes with at least ten starters. The same basic requirements must be met in order to attain the Amateur Field Champion title, except that all wins must come from Amateur stakes. Cocker Spaniels must also pass a noncompetitive water test consisting of a 20- to 30-yard retrieve before qualifying for a Field Champion title.

Chapter Twelve
Conformation Cockers

Do you watch the Westminster Dog Show and envision you and your Cocker parading around a similar ring? Showing a Cocker Spaniel can be very rewarding, but it also entails a lot of preparation—more than what most breeds require.

The most important preparation is making sure your Cocker is cut out to be a show dog. The truth is that unless your Cocker came from a pedigree of show dogs, with Champions (designated by a "Ch." in front of their names) within the first two generations, the chances are that she may not have the breeding required to meet the exacting points of the Cocker standard. If your breeder doesn't compete in dog shows, he or she probably did not choose your dog's parents with an eye toward producing a show dog. If, however, the breeder does compete in shows, ask her opinion of whether she thinks your dog is competitive.

Your Cocker may have been neutered or spayed, or sold to you with a limited registration, all of which would render your dog ineligible for conformation showing. The breeder is the only one who can change the limited registration to regular registration, so her opinion is again the first one you should seek.

Preparation also involves meticulous show grooming. It would be a rare pet groomer who could prepare a Cocker for show. Instead, you will almost certainly have to work with your breeder or pay a professional Cocker handler to give you grooming lessons.

Cocker Handling

You will need to learn to present your Cocker in the ring. Some breeds of dogs are shown mostly by their owners; unfortunately, Cockers tend to be shown by professional handlers. That means they are a difficult breed for a novice to start with. Because of that, most people new to the Cocker show world have a professional handler groom and show their dog for them, often sending the dog away to live with the handler.

Presentation of the Cocker is somewhat specialized, and the best Cocker handlers often show only Cockers. You can get an idea of who's who in Cocker handling by looking through a Cocker magazine.

how to strut around the ring, pose, and turn on the charm. You can practice posing your dog at home by placing her front legs parallel to each other and perpendicular to the ground, and her rear legs also parallel to each other with the hocks (the area from the rear ankle to the foot) perpendicular to the ground. Cockers are posed on a grooming table for the judge to examine, and on the floor in a lineup with the other dogs. Practice having your dog trot alertly in a straight line. Cockers are usually shown at a fairly fast trot, often on a barely tight lead. They are encouraged to trot a little ahead of the handler. More important than getting everything perfect is doing it all with a happy attitude, and you can help your dog keep this merry outlook through liberal handouts of treats.

A Cocker Championship

At a show, a judge will evaluate your Cocker in regard to type—that is, how well she exemplifies the areas of the standard that define a Cocker Spaniel as a Cocker Spaniel, such as head shape, coat, and overall proportions. She will also be evaluated on soundness, her ability to walk or trot in as efficient a manner as possible. Finally she'll be evaluated on temperament to check that she is not shy, aggressive, or sulky.

Attend a show and watch the handlers. Do they look professional in the ring? Do they exhibit good sportsmanship? Are their dogs well-groomed and well-trained? Don't stop there. Look at their grooming area and vehicle. Are the dogs happy? Are the handlers treating them gently? Do they seem to like their dogs? Is their setup safe? Would you feel secure sending your dog to stay with them? Finally, talk to them after they are through showing. Inquire about rates, being sure to ask if additional costs apply to grooming, board, splitting of expenses, or bonuses. Make sure you understand what they expect from you.

But maybe you really want to do it yourself. Often a local kennel club, which you can locate through the AKC, will sponsor conformation classes. Here your Cocker will learn

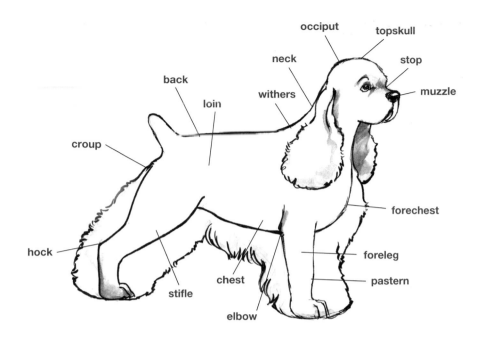

External anatomy.

If she ranks high in comparison to her competition, she may win points toward her championship.

Points are awarded to the top dog of either sex that's not already a champion; from 1 to 5 points can be won at each show according to the number of dogs defeated. To become an AKC champion, she needs to win 15 points, including twice winning at least 3 points at once. If she is judged the best non-champion of her sex, she will also compete for the best of variety: Black, ASCOB, or Parti. That winner goes on to compete in the Sporting group, the winner of which competes with the six other group winners for Best in Show.

Most other breeds compete for Best of Breed instead of Best of Variety, but Cockers compete only for Best of Breed at independent specialties, which are shows held only for Cocker Spaniels. In that case the three variety winners compete against each other for Best of Breed.

Even if you leave the show ribbonless, you'll have lots of company; just don't let your Cocker know and make sure you enjoy the day for what it should be: a fun outing with your dog where you can meet other Cocker Spaniel lovers.

The expression is "intelligent, alert, soft, and appealing."

The AKC Cocker Spaniel Standard

The current Cocker Spaniel standard was approved in 1992. The complete standard can be found on the American Spaniel Club homepage. The following is a synopsis of it.

General. The Cocker Spaniel is sturdy and compact, capable of considerable speed and great endurance. His head is cleanly chiseled and refined. He must be free and merry, sound, well-balanced throughout and in action show a keen inclination to work.

Height at the Withers. Males 15 inches; females 14 inches, plus or minus a half inch. If the dog is more than a half inch taller than the ideal for its sex, it is disqualified; more than a half inch shorter, it is severely penalized.

The length of the body from the breastbone to back of the thigh is slightly longer than the distance from the highest point of the withers to the ground.

Expression: intelligent, alert, soft, and appealing.

Eyes: Slightly almond shaped, full, and looking directly forward, dark brown in color.

Ears: Long and lobular, placed no higher than a line to the lower part of the eye. The leather is fine and the ear is well-feathered.

Skull: Rounded, with clearly defined eyebrows and a pronounced stop.

Muzzle: Broad and deep, with square jaws. Well-chiseled beneath

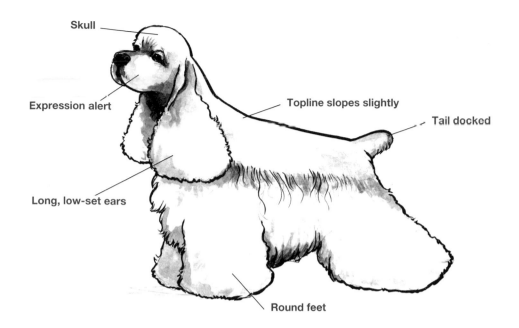

Skull

Expression alert

Long, low-set ears

Topline slopes slightly

Tail docked

Round feet

Some points of the Standard.

the eyes with no prominence in the cheeks. The distance from the stop to the tip of the nose is one-half the distance from the stop up over the crown to the base of the skull.

Nose: Well-developed nostrils, black in color in dogs with black as part of their coat color; in other colors it harmonizes with the eye rims, and may be brown, liver, or black (the darker the better).

Lips: Full upper lip of sufficient depth to cover the lower jaw.

Teeth: Strong, meeting in a scissors bite.

Neck: Long enough to allow the nose to reach the ground easily, muscular and free from pendulous "throatiness." It rises strongly from

the shoulders and arches slightly as it tapers to join the head.

Topline: Sloping slightly toward the rear.

Chest: Deep, reaching at least to the elbows. Wide enough for adequate heart and lung space, but not so wide as to interfere with the straight, forward movement of the forelegs. Ribs are deep and well-sprung.

Back: Strong, sloping slightly downward from the shoulders to the set-on of the tail.

Tail: Docked, set-on and carried on a line with the topline of the back, or slightly higher; never straight up and never so low as to indicate timidity. When the dog is moving the tail action is merry.

Shoulders: Well laid back, forming an angle with the upper arm of approximately 90 degrees. When viewed from the side with the forelegs vertical, the elbow is directly below the highest point of the shoulder blade.

Forelegs: Parallel, straight, and strongly boned, set close to the body.

Pasterns: Short and strong. Dewclaws may be removed.

Feet: Compact, large, round, and firm with horny pads; they turn neither in nor out.

Hips: Wide, with quarters well-rounded and muscular.

Hind legs: Strongly boned, and muscled with powerful thighs. Moderate angulation at the stifle, which is strong and has no slippage.

Hocks: Strong and low. Dewclaws may be removed.

Coat. Short and fine on the head; medium length on the body. Well-feathered on the ears, chest, abdomen, and legs, but not so excessively that it obscures the dog's lines or affects its movement or function. Texture is silky, flat, or slightly wavy. Excessive coat or curly or cottony-textured coat shall be severely penalized.

Trimming for show. Use of electric clippers on the back coat is not desirable. Trimming to enhance the dog's true lines should be done to appear as natural as possible.

Color and Markings

• Black Variety: Solid black, or black with tan points. Shadings of brown or liver in the coat are not desirable. A small amount of white on the chest

Disqualifications

Height: Males over 15½ inches; females over 14½ inches.

Color and Markings: The aforementioned colors are the only acceptable colors or combination of colors. Any other colors or combination of colors will disqualify.

Black Variety: White markings except on chest and throat.

Any Solid Color Other Than Black Variety: White markings except on chest and throat.

Parti-color Variety: Primary color 90 percent or more.

Tan Points: (1) Tan markings in excess of 10 percent; (2) absence of tan markings in Black or ASCOB Variety in any of the specified locations in an otherwise tan-pointed dog.

and/or throat is allowed; white in any other location shall disqualify.

• ASCOB Variety: Any solid color other than black, ranging from lightest cream to darkest red, including brown and brown with tan points. The color shall be uniform, but lighter color of the feathering is permissible. A small amount of white on the chest and/or throat is allowed; white in any other location shall disqualify.

• Parti-color Variety: White with one or more other allowed colors, or roan, with or without tan points. Primary color which is ninety percent or more shall disqualify.

Tan points: In the case of tan points in the Black or ASCOB vari-

Parti-color over dark buff.

ety, the markings shall be located as follows:

1. A clear tan spot over each eye;

2. On the sides of the muzzle and on the cheeks;

3. On the underside of the ears;

4. On all feet and/or legs;

5. Under the tail;

6. On the chest, optional; presence or absence shall not be penalized.

Tan markings that are not readily visible or that amount only to traces shall be penalized. Tan on the muzzle that extends upward, over, and joins shall also be penalized. The absence of tan markings in the Black or ASCOB variety in any of the specified locations in any otherwise tan-pointed dog shall disqualify. Tan points in excess of 10 percent of the dog's color shall disqualify.

Gait. Ground-covering, smooth, and effortless, driving with powerful rear quarters and reaching with the forequarters to counterbalance the rear force.

Temperament. Equable, with no suggestion of timidity.

Chapter Thirteen

Color Me Cocker

Cockers come in three color varieties, but many more colors—not all of which are acceptable according to the standard—exist if you plan to breed, you should understand Cocker color genetics. Even if you don't plant to breed, it's fun to figure out how genes determine your dog's color.

Coat Color and Genetics

Your Cocker Spaniel's color depends on the interaction of many genes, some of which mask the actions of others and some of which modify the action of others.

Solid vs. Sable vs. Tan-Pointed (A, a^y, a^t): The **A** locus has two or three possible alleles found in Cocker Spaniels. The discrepancy lies in the fact that a new theory regarding dominant black has recently been accepted by many geneticists. Traditionally, the most dominant of these alleles, **A**, allows for a solid-colored dog, such as a

Buff versus non-buff. The black dog has at least one copy of the E gene.

black (or brown or blue, depending on other modifiers). Next in dominance is a^y, which produces red coloration as long as no **A** allele is present. Most recessive is a^t, which produces tan-pointed markings as long as neither **A** nor are a^y are present. The typical tan-pointed pattern has tan above the eyes, on the cheeks and sides of the muzzle, on the underside of the ears, on all feet and possibly legs, under the tail, and possibly on the chest.

The newer scheme contends that dominant black is found on a separate locus, **K**. The presence of **K** makes the base coat color black before genes at other loci modify it. The recessive, **k,** makes the coat some shade of red, depending on other modifiers.

In either case, a^y codes for red or sable. Some breeders contend that a dog that is a^y a^y will be a clear red. However, a dog with one copy of a^y and one copy of a^t will be sabled, which consists of black hairs overlying red or buff ones.

Even if a dog has genes that code for producing black, they can be prevented from being black because of alleles in the **E** series.

Cockers come in three color varieties, but many more colors.

Buff vs. non-buff (E, e): This gene affects the color that is already determined by the **A** series. The **E** allele allows black or brown pigment (if coded for by other genes) to be expressed However, if a dog has two recessive **e** alleles, the hair is prevented from forming black or brown pigment no matter what. Such a dog will be some shade of buff, from dark red to pale cream.

Black vs. Brown (B, b): The allele for black pigmentation (**B**) is domi- nant over that for brown (**b**) pigmentation. A black dog may or may not carry a hidden **b** allele, but has at least one **B** allele. Brown, also called liver or chocolate, occurs only when a dog has two copies of the recessive **b** allele. Brown dogs have a liver-colored nose and lighter-colored eyes, nails, and foot pads.

Black vs. Blue (D, d): Blue (or gray) is a dilution of black caused by the presence of two recessive **d** alleles. It appears to be rare in Cockers and is not accepted by the breed standard.

Light vs. Dark Buff (C, c^{ch}, c^e): Alleles at this location determine how dark a buff-colored dog is, from dark red through pale cream. The most dominant in the series produces darker shades, the intermediate (c^{ch}) produces intermediate shades, and the most recessive (c^e) produces the lightest shades. This is probably an oversimplification, and combinations of them almost certainly produce more variations.

Solid vs. Spotted (S, s^p, s^e): Alleles at this location affect the amount of white on a dog, with more dominant alleles producing dogs with less white. The **S** allele produces a solid dog, the **s^p** allele produces the normal parti-color pattern, and **s^e** produces a dog with very few patches of color at all. Combinations of different alleles produce intermediate amounts of white. Think of the white as being poured over the pattern the dog would normally have. White tends to begin at the places on the body where color pigment migrates to last during development, so if only a little white is present, it's usually on the feet, tail tip, and chest.

Roan vs. Non-Roan (R, r): Roan refers to white hairs interspersed among a darker base color. The dominant allele, **R**, produces roan, so that, with the exception of a rare mutation, a roan must have at least one roan parent.

Ticked vs. Non-ticked (T, t): Most noticeable in parti-colors, ticking refers to the small dots of color seen

What the Standard Says

The Black variety should be jet black, with or without tan points. A small amount of white on the chest and throat is allowed, but if it appears in any other location it's a disqualification.

The ASCOB variety is any solid color other than black, from light cream to buff to dark red and every shade in between, plus brown (or liver) with or without tan points. It should be of a uniform shade, with allowances for slightly lighter feathering. White is permissible to the same extent as in the black variety.

The Parti-color variety is made up of white plus at least one other color, such as black, cream, buff, red, brown, or roan, with or without tan points. The colors should be well separated by white, with white covering at least 10 percent of the coat. Parti-colors also include solid roans, which are a combination of dark and white hairs.

against a white background. It is not to be confused with roan, and has no relationship to roan. The dominant allele, **T**, allows ticking to occur.

Merle vs. Non-Merle (M, m): Merle refers to a pattern consisting of ragged blotches of diluted color interspersed among full color. It acts on either black or brown to produce either blue or red diluted areas; however, it does not affect the tan on tan-pointed dogs. It may affect the iris color of the eye, so merles often

Darker buff colors tend to be dominant over lighter ones.

have blue or partially blue eyes. It takes only one copy of the dominant **M** allele to create a merle dog. If a dog has two copies of the **M** allele, it tends to have patches of white and, more importantly, visual and auditory problems. Such double-merles may be blind or deaf.

DNA Tests for Color

A DNA test is available that can discover the presence of recessive **b** and **e** alleles. That means you can find out if your black (or black and tan, or black parti, or black tri) could produce brown or buff offspring. It will also tell you if your brown (or brown and tan, or brown parti) could pro-

duce buff- or red-colored offspring. If your dog is buff or buff parti, or red or red parti, the test will tell you whether he carries alleles for black or for brown. The test is offered by VetGen (*www.vetgen.com/cockcolor.html*) and by HealthGene (*www.health gene.com/canine/C128_spaniel_ame rican_cocker.asp*).

The Sable Story

Few, if any, Cocker colors have aroused as much controversy as sable. Sable refers to red or tan color with black hairs interspersed throughout them, especially along the back, face, and lower ears. The color is first mentioned in 1938 in a

Parti-color, or white spotting, can be overlaid over any other pattern, in this case a black and tan.

science journal dealing with heredity. The author mentions the existence of three unrelated sable Cocker Spaniels, each from families in which sable had not been reported previously. In subsequent years controversy ensued concerning whether sable was a legitimate color. Detractors of the color said it had no past history in the breed, whereas proponents speculated that the many dogs described as "mahogany reds" were really sables. In fact, in the 1920s through the 1940s a handful of Cockers were registered as sables (or using terms clearly describing sables, such as "tan with black ears").

In the early years the standard did not include exact descriptions of the colors allowed in each variety. When a few sables were shown in the 1970s, they were classed as ASCOBs, and several of them finished championships. However, the

ASCOB

In 1944 the solid colors were separated into Black and ASCOB varieties, so three Cocker varieties represented the breed in the Sporting group. The following year, 1945, the first ASCOB, a buff named Ch. Stockdale Town Talk, won Best in Show at the prestigious Westminster Kennel Club, an important event in creating interest in the color.

In early years brown (or liver) Cockers were often destroyed at birth, perhaps because they were reminiscent of liver spaniel breeds such as Field Spaniels or Sussex Spaniels.

voted out, but again, not without controversy regarding wording. In 1992 the wording of the standard was changed so that sable was not included as an allowable color. A petition in 1997 to allow sables back received a majority vote, but not the two thirds needed for approval.

At present, sables cannot compete in AKC conformation events, but can compete in all other AKC events. Many people still breed and own sable Cocker Spaniels, and hope they will one day be fully accepted. Other Cocker fanciers are suspicious that they represent impure breeding, and feel the breed has enough color variation already. For an in-depth discussion of the situation, and to join other sable enthusiasts, visit *www.sable-cocker.com*.

standard for ASCOB was subsequently clarified in a way that excluded sables. The parti-color description did not include that clarification, so sable and whites could be shown, leading to confusion on the part of many judges as to whether they were acceptable.

Around 1990 the American Spaniel Club attempted to clarify the situation by specifically describing each color pattern allowed in each color variety. A ballot was sent to the membership asking whether sables should be allowed to be shown as ASCOBs and partis, or whether they should be disqualified. Controversy over the way ballots were counted and the resulting proposed wording in the standard led to a second vote in which sables were

The Merle Mix-up

Merle has never been an accepted Cocker color, but that doesn't mean Merle dogs don't exist. However, it seems that their appearance is fairly new, leading to supposition that they have resulted from a cross to another breed in which merle occurs. The problem with merles is that breeding two of them together produces, on average, one-quarter offspring that are MM. These so-called "double-merles" often have vision and hearing problems, so breeders try to avoid producing them. However, sometimes it can be difficult to tell if a dog is a merle, especially if it is a roan or sable merle where the merle can be

A chocolate and tan, and a solid chocolate puppy. Both carry two copies of the b gene. The chocolate and tan puppy also carries two copies of the a^t gene.

lost among the already irregular coat pattern. Unfortunately, many merle owners register their dogs as roans because the Cocker registration form doesn't include merle as a color choice. Merles are not roans. For more information on merles, go to *www.merlecockcr.com.*

Mismarks

Mismarks in Cockers refer to areas of white that appear where the standard does not allow them. Solid-colored Cockers are allowed no more white than a small bit on the chest and throat. If it appears elsewhere it's a disqualification. Why not show them as parti-colors? Because parti-colored Cockers must have at least 10 percent white. That means a dog with long streaks of white on the neck and chest, or with a blaze, or with white feet or toes, has too much white to be a solid yet not enough white to be a parti. This is why solids and parti-colors are not usually bred together.

Rare Colors?

Some Cocker colors are more common than others, and some, such as merle and sable, are fairly uncommon (as well as not accepted). No color should demand a higher price than another. Breeders who produce puppies with color as a priority have their priorities mixed up. Health, temperament, conformation, and field ability are the goals good breeders strive toward, not unusual colors.

Cocker Spaniel Resources

Organizations

American Spaniel Club
P.O. Box 4194
Frankfort, KY 40604-4194
502-352-4290
E-mail: ASC.Secretary@gmail.com
www.asc-cockerspaniel.org

Local Cocker Spaniel Clubs
*www.asc-cockerspaniel.org/asc/
    memberclub.asp*

American Spaniel Club Foundation
*www.asc-cockerspaniel.org/ascf/
    purpose.asp*

American Cocker Spaniel Club of
    Great Britain
http://acscgb.tripod.com/

Great Lakes American Cocker
    Spaniel Hunting Enthusiasts
*http://userpages.chorus.net/
    hunsaker/glacshe.html*

American Kennel Club (AKC)
5580 Centerview Drive
Raleigh, NC 27606-3390
www.akc.org

Other National All-Breed Clubs

*http://www.canadasguidetodogs.com/
    nationalclubs.htm*

Canine Health Foundation
www.akcchf.org

Orthopedic Foundation for Animals
2300 Nifong Boulevard
Columbia, MO 65201
www.offa.org

Therapy Dogs International
88 Bartley Road
Flanders, NJ 07836
www.tdi-dog.org

North American Flyball Association
P.O. Box 8
Mount Hope, ON L0R 1W0

Rescue

American Society for the Prevention
    of Cruelty to Animals (ASPCA)
Hotline: (888) 426-4435
(A consultation fee may be charged.)

Petfinder
www.petfinder.com

List of Local Cocker Rescue Groups
www.asc-cockerspaniel.org/breed/
rescuegroups.asp

Periodicals
Animal Network
www.animalnetwork.com

The American Cocker Magazine
14531 Jefferson Street, Dept CP
Midway City, CA 92655
(714) 893-0053
www.cyberpet.com/cyberdog/
products/pubmag/premier.html

The Cocker Classic
(503) 701-7974
www.cockerclassic.com

Dog World Magazine
www.dogworldmag.com

Purebred Dogs
www.akc.org

Spaniels in the Field Magazine
5312 Wolf Knoll Road
Orr, MN 55771
www.spanielsinthefield.com

Many old issues of Cocker magazines now out of print can be found on Internet sites such as e-Bay. Look for *The Cocker Spaniel Leader, Cocker Visitor, Wagging Tail,* and the *American Cocker Spaniel Review.*

Puppies of one color variety can be born to parents of another, as with this black variety (black and tan) puppy and its ASCOB (buff) parent.

Books

Austin, Norman, and Jean Austin. *The Complete American Cocker Spaniel.* New York: Howell, 1993.

Coile, D. Caroline. *Beyond Fetch: Fun, Interactive Activities for You and Your Dog.* New York: Wiley, 2003.

Coile, D. Caroline. *Show Me! A Dog Showing Primer.* Hauppauge, NY: Barron's Educational Series, 1997.

Cole, Robert. *You Be the Judge: The Cocker Spaniel.* Wenatchee, WA: Dogwise, 2002.

Gordoner, Bill, and Lloyd Alton. *The World of the Cocker Spaniel.* Neptune City, NJ: TFH, 1994.

Grossman, Alvin. *The American Cocker Spaniel.* Sun City, AZ: Doral, 2000.

Scott, John Paul, and John L. Fuller. *Genetics and the Social Behavior*

Spaniel Web Sites

American Cocker Spaniel Pictures	http://thebrycegroup.com/american_cocker_spaniel/
Cocker Spaniel Online Magazine	www.cockerspaniels.com
Cocker Spaniel Standard Comparisons	www.canadasguidetodogs.com/spaniel/am_breedchart.htm
Gun Dog Magazine Online	www.gundogmag.com
Gun Dogs Online	www.gundogsonline.com
Pedigrees	http://www.cockers-online.se/
Pedigrees	www.cockerspaniels.com/pedigree/pedigree.htm
Pedigrees	www.showcockers.com/PedigreeInfo.html
Show Cockers Online	www.showcockers.com
The Spaniel Journal	www.spanieljournal.com
Spaniels in the Field	www.spanielsinthefield.com

Web Pages

Animal CPR	http://members.aol.com/henryhbk/acpr.html
Infodog Dog Show Site	www.infodog.com
Lost Pet Information	http://lostapet.org/missing_dogs.html
Rally Obedience	www.rallyobedience.com
The Dog Agility Page	http://www.dogpatch.org/agility/
Dr. P's Dog Training Links	http://www.uwsp.edu/acad/psych/dog/dog.htm

of Dogs. Chicago: University of Chicago Press, 1965.

Spencer, James. *Hup! Training Spaniels the American Way.* Loveland, CO: Alpine, 2002.

For a list of publications issued by the American Spaniel Club, go to: *www.asc-cockerspaniel.org.*

For a list of hunting books got to: *www.spanieljournal.com/shop.html.*

For other Cocker books and items go to: *www.asc-cockerspaniel.org/shop/index.asp.*

Videos

AKC Breed Standard Video
www.akc.org/store/

In the Ribbons: Cocker Spaniel
Canine Training Systems
www.dogwise.com

Show Grooming the Cocker Spaniel
Sonnen Productions
www.dogwise.com

Pet Grooming the Sporting Types
Sonnen Productions
www.dogwise.com

Index

It's a dog's life, Cocker-style.